The Allegro Appassionato Book

for Cello

by Cassia Harvey

based on Allegro Appassionato
by Camille Saint-Saëns

Grateful thanks to cellist/teacher Colin Hartwick and cellist Alex Steketee
for their help with the editing process!

CHP370

©2020 by C. Harvey Publications All Rights Reserved.

www.charveypublications.com - print books
www.learnstrings.com - PDF downloadable books
www.harveystringarrangements.com - chamber music

Table of Contents

	Page
How this Book Works	3

Allegro Appassionato Exercises

	Page
Section One, Bowing No. 1 (measures 1-12)	4
Section One, Bowing No. 2 (measures 1-12)	8
Section Two (measures 13-36)	14
Section Three (measures 37-61)	20
Section Four, Bowing No. 1 (measures 62-92)	29
Section Four, Bowing No. 2 (measures 62-92)	30
Section Five (measures 93-116	48
Section Six (measures 117-133)	52
Section Seven (measures 134-156)	54
Section Eight, Bowing No. 1 (measures 157-168)	64
Section Eight, Bowing No. 2 (measures 157-168)	64
Section Nine, Bowing No. 1 (measures 169-183)	65
Section Nine, Bowing No. 2 (measures 169-183)	65
Section Ten (measures 184-215)	82

Complete Piece

	Page
Bowing No. 1	92
Bowing No. 2	96

How this Book Works

This book divides *Allegro Appassionato*, by Camille Saint-Saëns, into short sections and provides exercises for mastering each section.

Each exercise was written to teach a specific skill. Shifts are often repeated to help with acquiring muscle memory. Double stops are included for establishing relative pitch, building left-hand strength, and balancing the bow across two strings. Most of the bowing work focuses on the agility and speed necessary to play the piece well. Rhythm is often taught by subdividing longer notes into shorter beats. In some cases, small "guide notes" are included above the printed notes to help with rhythm.

Vibrato may be used throughout the book as soon as intonation is secure. Playing the exercises with vibrato will help balance the hand over the notes being played and will also help develop tone.

Roman numerals refer to strings (never positions).
I = A string   III = G string
II = D string IV = C string

Some preparatory books and pieces to **study before** this book:
- Fifth Position for the Cello: CHP198
- Tenor Clef for the Cello: CHP109
- The Romberg Sonata in C Major Study Book for Cello: CHP348
- Tarantella by W. H. Squire
- The Swan Study Book for Cello: CHP346

Some books and pieces to **study along with** this book:
- Learning Three-Octave Scales on the Cello: CHP356
- Shifting in Keys for Cello, Book One: CHP244
- Bowing Studies on Arpeggios for Cello, Book One: CHP222
- Finger Exercises for the Cello, Book Three: CHP142

Some books and pieces to **study after** this book:
- The Faure Elegie Study Book for Cello: CHP319
- Thumb Position School for the Cello: CHP261
- Learning Three-Octave Arpeggios on the Cello: CHP359
- The Saint-Saëns Cello Concerto No. 1 Study Book, Volume One: CHP349

4

The Allegro Appassionato Study Book for Cello

Roman numerals refer to strings:
I = A string
II = D string
III = G string
IV = C string

Allegro Appassionato
Section One: Measures 1-12 - Bowing No. 1

Solo by Camille Saint-Saëns
Exercises by Cassia Harvey

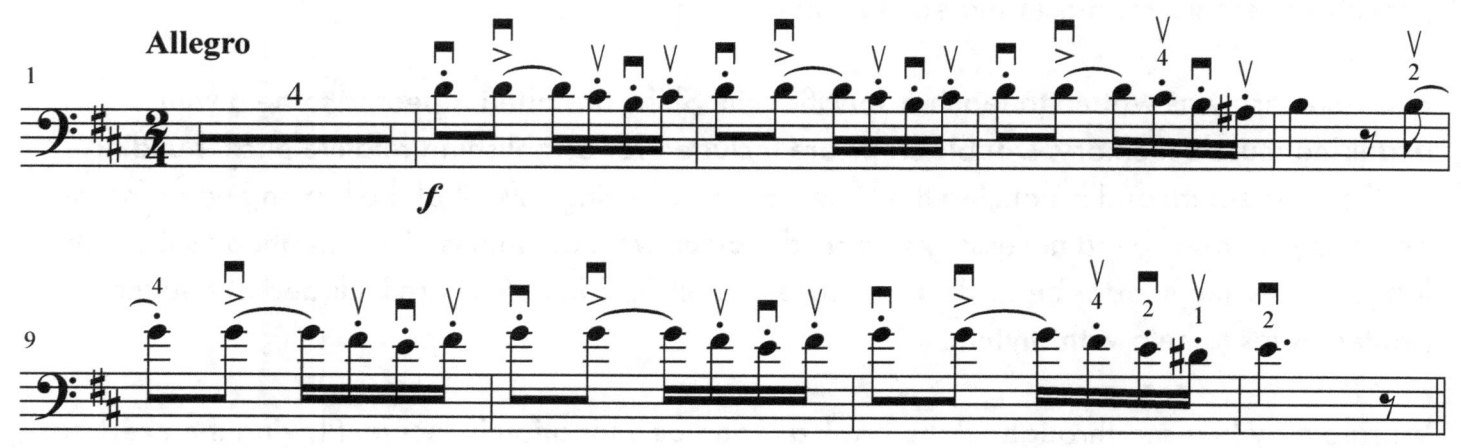

1. Learning the Shifts
Measures 1-12

©2020 C. Harvey Publications All Rights Reserved.

2. Shifting Back from Fourth Position: Measures 8-12

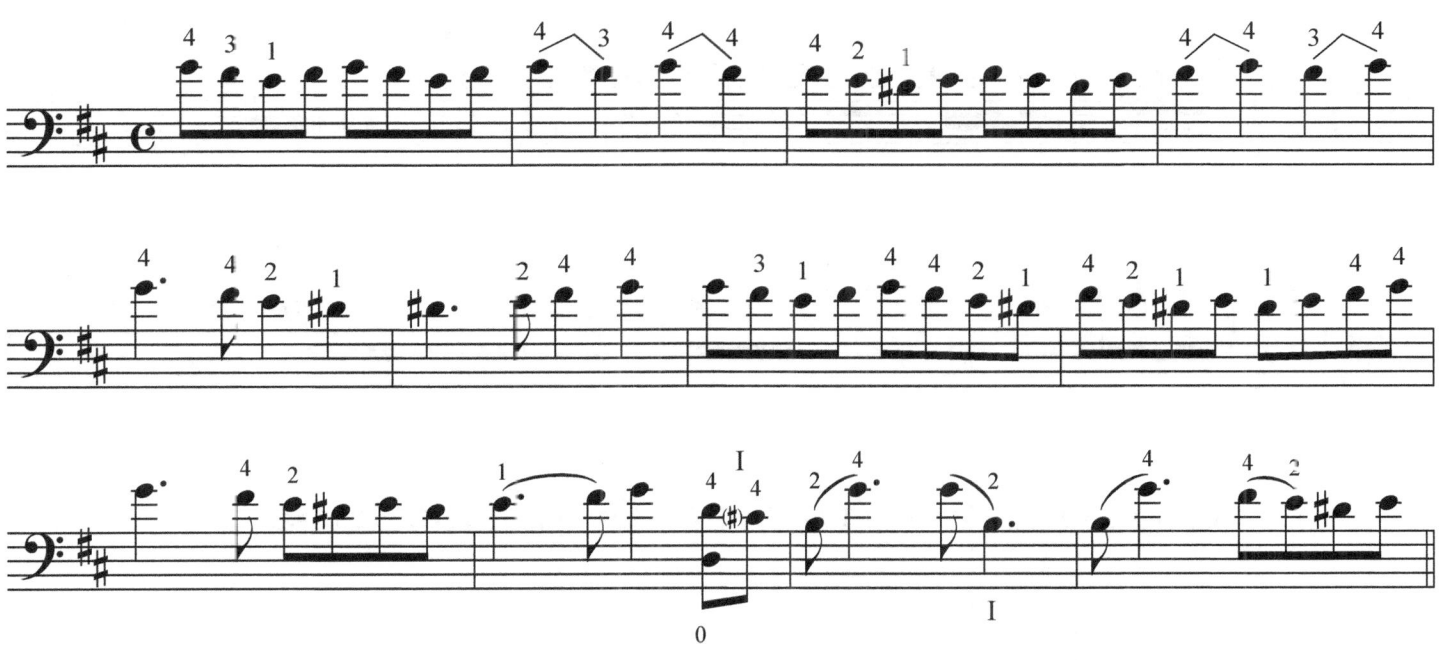

3. Retaking Bows - Bowing No. 1: Measures 5-12

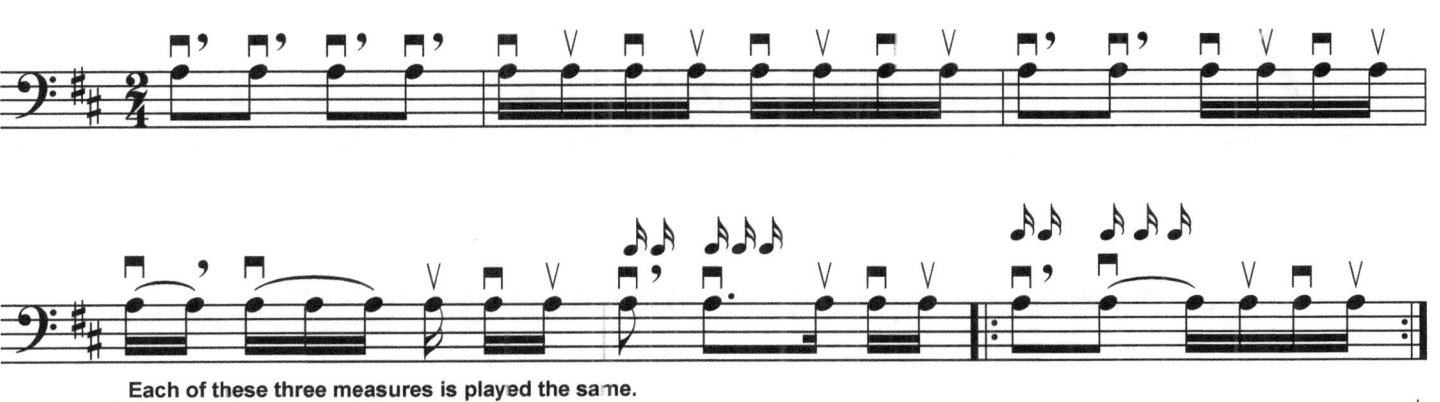

Each of these three measures is played the same.

4. Accents - Bowing No. 1: Measures 5-12

5. Rhythmically Retaking - **Bowing No. 1:** Measures 5-12

6. Feeling the Underlying Rhythm - **Bowing No. 1:** Measures 5-12

7. Retaking and Underlying Rhythm - **Bowing No. 1:** Measures 5-12

©2020 C. Harvey Publications All Rights Reserved.

8. Staccato for Rhythm - **Bowing No. 1:** Measures 5-12

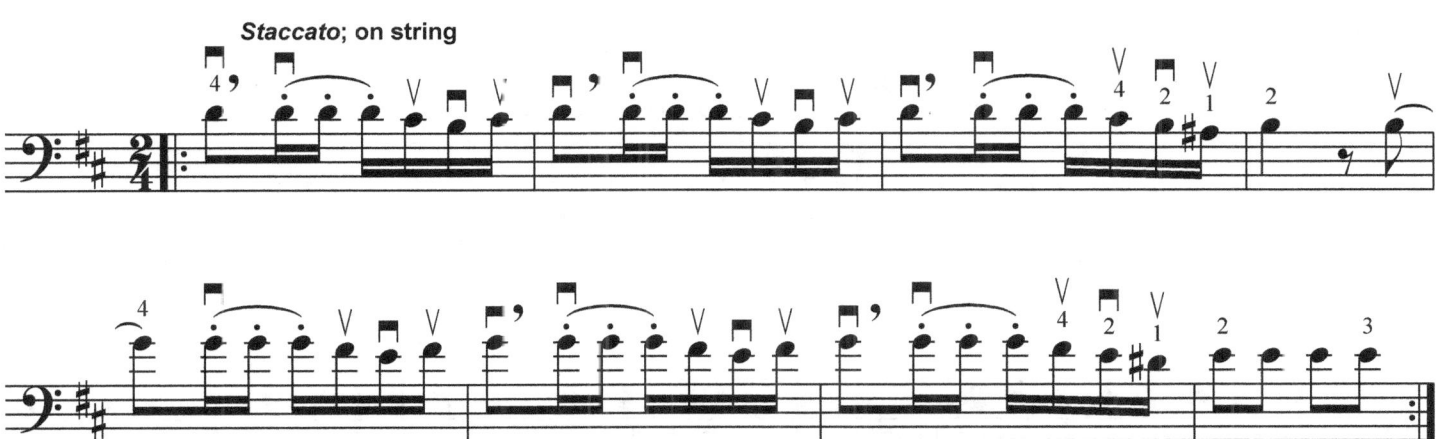

9. More Staccato for Rhythm - **Bowing No. 1:** Measures 5-12

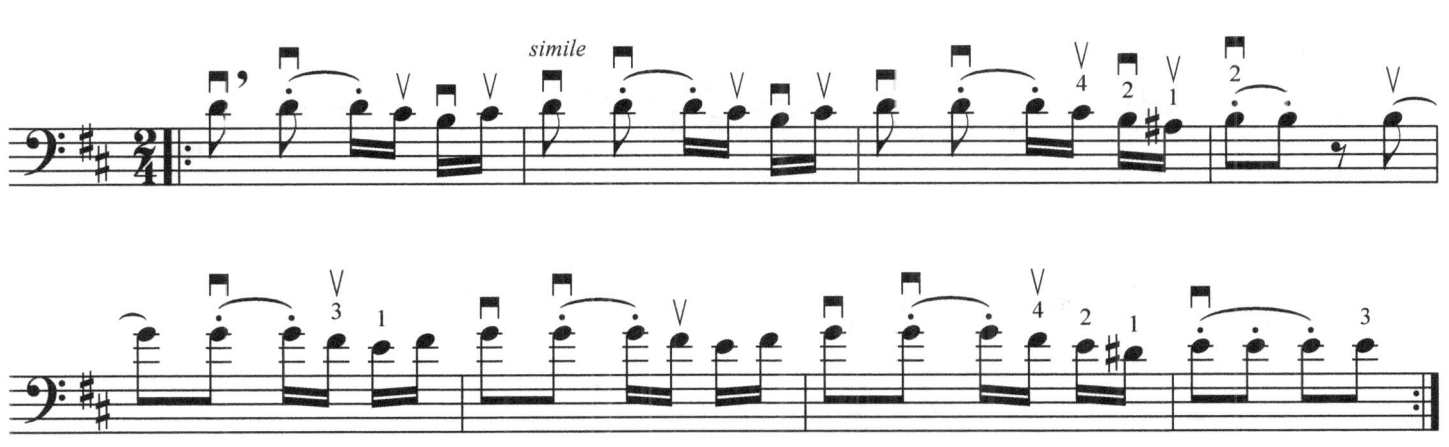

10. Introduction and Solo Entrance - **Bowing No. 1:** Measures 5-12

11. Spiccato - **Bowing No. 1:** Measures 5-12

Optional: Spiccato
Many recorded interpretations of this opening treat the sixteenth note articulation dots as meaning "light" rather than "off the string." If you wish to play these notes off the string, make sure the last down bow before the sixteenth notes in each measure only reaches 1/4-1/3 of the bow so that you will be near the balance point of the bow and spiccato will be an option.

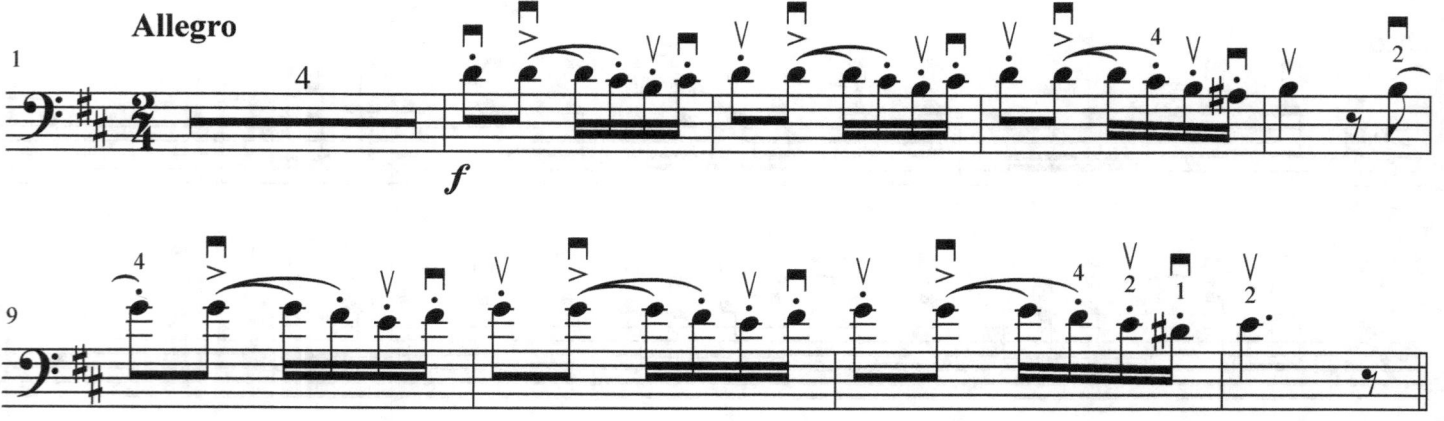

Allegro Appassionato
Section One: Measures 1-12 - Bowing No. 2

The Allegro Appassionato Study Book for Cello

12. Retaking and Hooking Bows - **Bowing No. 2:** Measures 5-12

Both measures are played the same.

Staccato; on string

Both measures are played the same.

13. Accents - **Bowing No. 2:** Measures 5-12

©2020 C. Harvey Publications All Rights Reserved.

14. The Underlying Rhythm - **Bowing No. 2:** Measures 5-12

15. Hooked Bows - **Bowing No. 2:** Measures 5-12

16. Staccato for Rhythm I - **Bowing No. 2:** Measures 5-12

©2020 C. Harvey Publications   All Rights Reserved.

17. Staccato for Rhythm II - **Bowing No. 2:** Measures 5-12

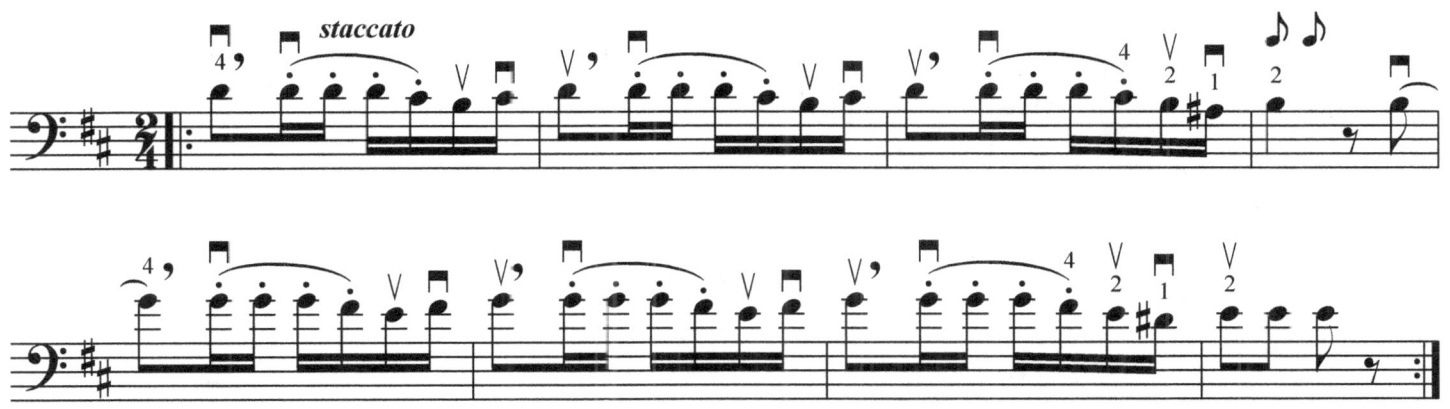

18. Staccato for Rhythm III - **Bowing No. 2:** Measures 5-12

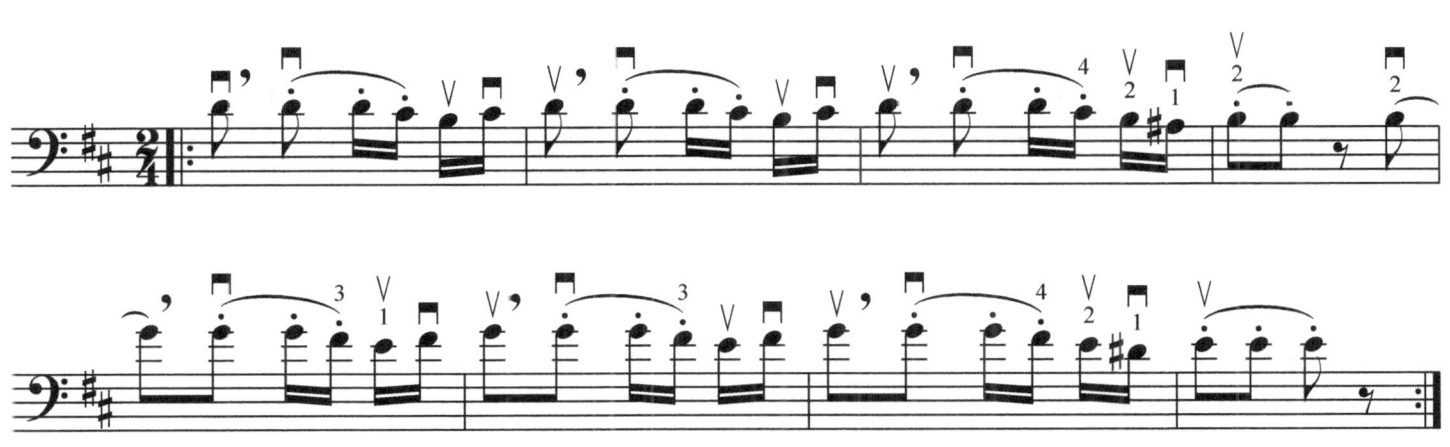

19. Introduction and Solo Entrance - **Bowing No. 2:** Measures 5-12

20. Spiccato - Bowing No. 2: Measures 5-12

Optional: Spiccato

Many recorded interpretations of this opening treat the sixteenth note articulation dots as meaning "light" rather than "off the string." If you wish to play these notes off the string, make sure the last down bow before the sixteenth notes in each measure only reaches 1/4-1/3 of the bow so that you will be near the balance point of the bow and spiccato will be an option.

The Allegro Appassionato Study Book for Cello

13

21. Playing With the Accompaniment - **Bowing No. 1:** Measures 5-12

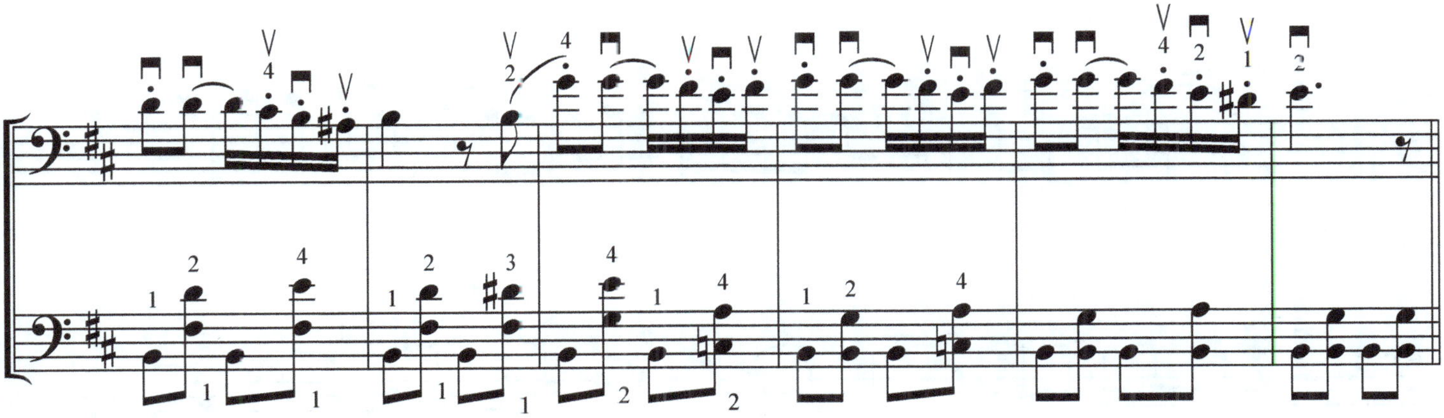

22. Playing With the Accompaniment - **Bowing No. 2:** Measures 5-12

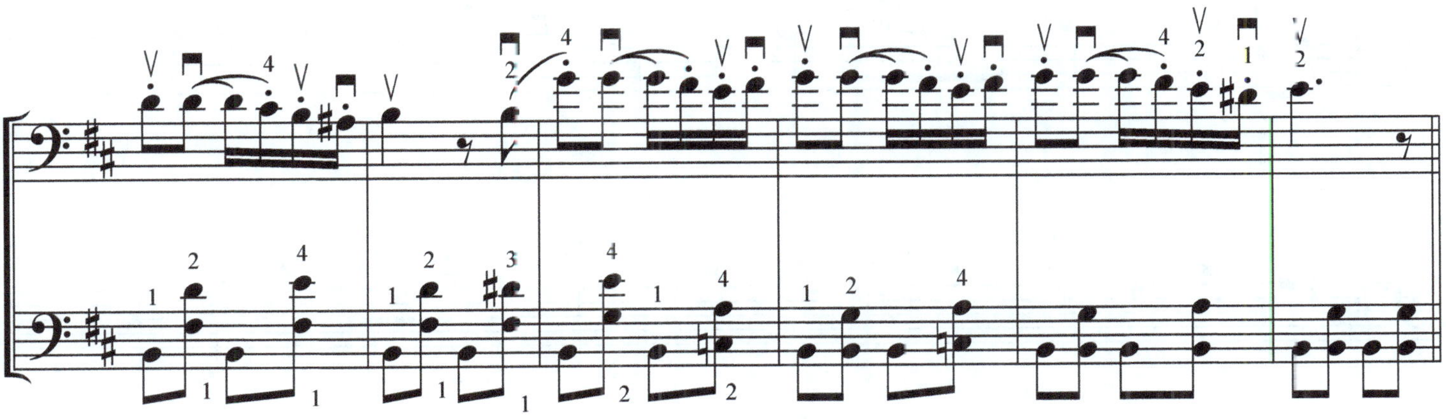

©2020 C. Harvey Publications All Rights Reserved.

Allegro Appassionato
Section Two: Measures 13-36

23. Learning the Notes: Measures 11-16

The Allegro Appassionato Study Book for Cello

24. Shifting: Measures 11-16

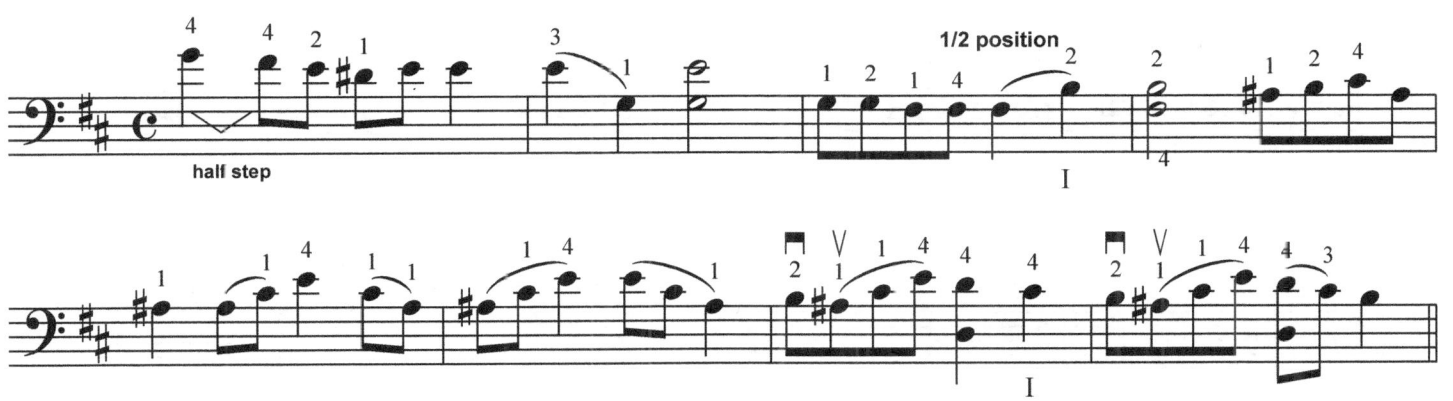

25. Learning the Notes: Measures 17-20

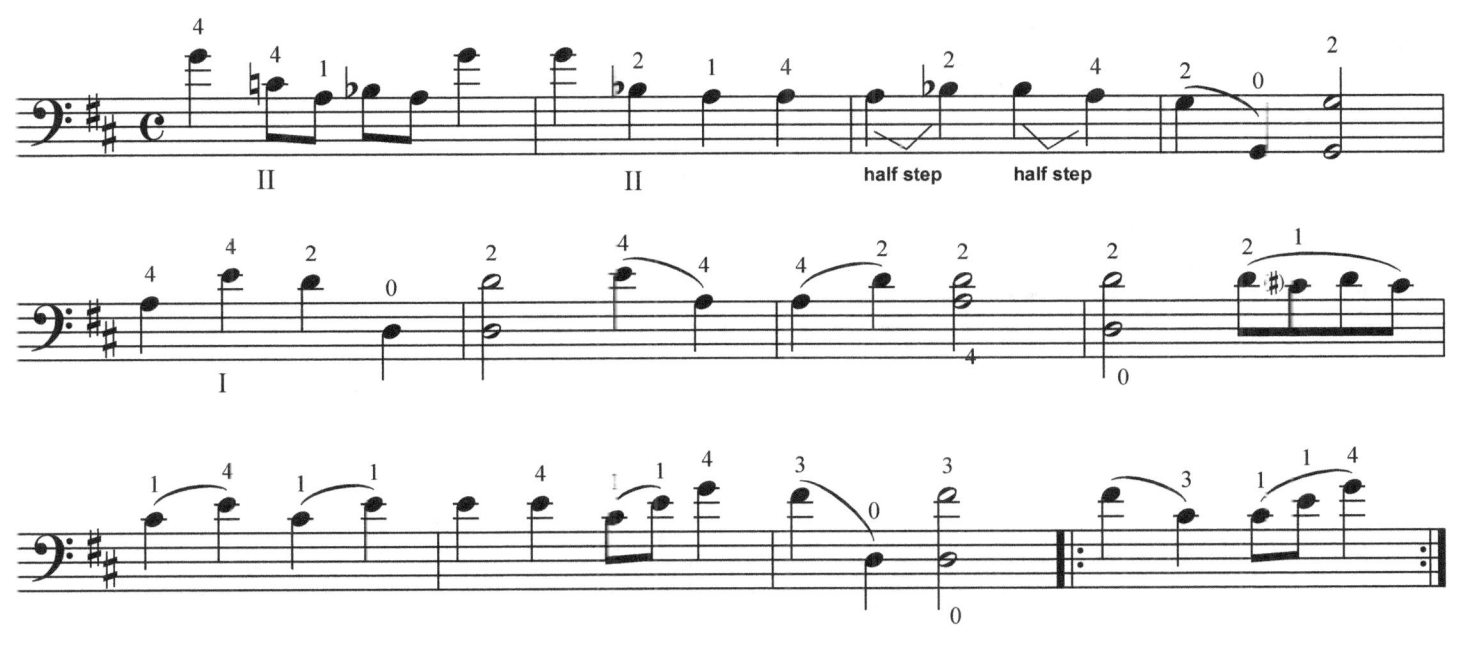

26. Intonation: Measures 13-20

©2020 C. Harvey Publications All Rights Reserved.

27. Rhythm: Measures 11-20

28. Rhythm Duet: Measures 13-20

The Allegro Appassionato Study Book for Cello

29. Shifting and Rhythm: Measures 21-28

30. Learning the Notes: Measures 29-32

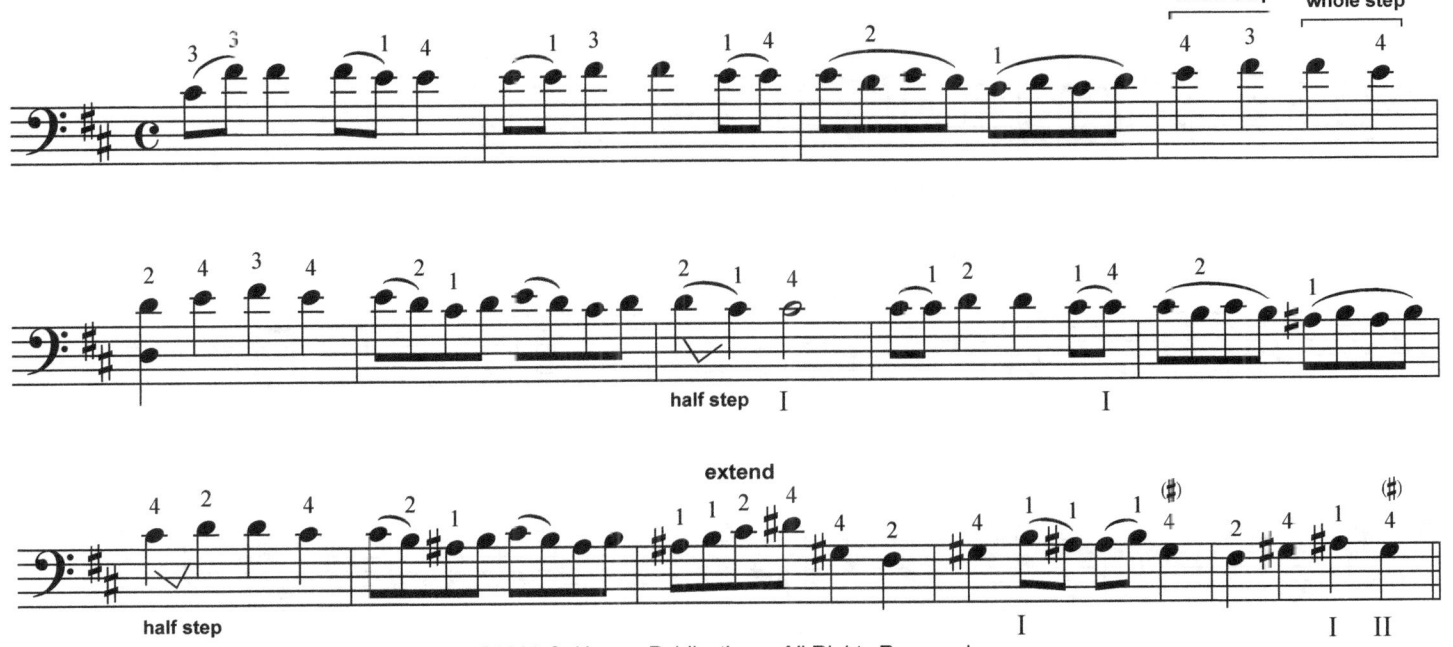

©2020 C. Harvey Publications All Rights Reserved.

The Allegro Appassionato Study Book for Cello

32a. Shifting, Top Fingering: Measures 29-36

32b. Shifting, Bottom Fingering: Measures 29-36

©2020 C. Harvey Publications All Rights Reserved.

Allegro Appassionato
Section Three: Measures 37-61

The Allegro Appassionato Study Book for Cello

33. Double Stops: Measures 37-38, 45-46

©2020 C. Harvey Publications All Rights Reserved.

The Allegro Appassionato Study Book for Cello

34. Tenor Clef: Measures 37-38

35. Learning the Notes: Measures 37-40, 45-48

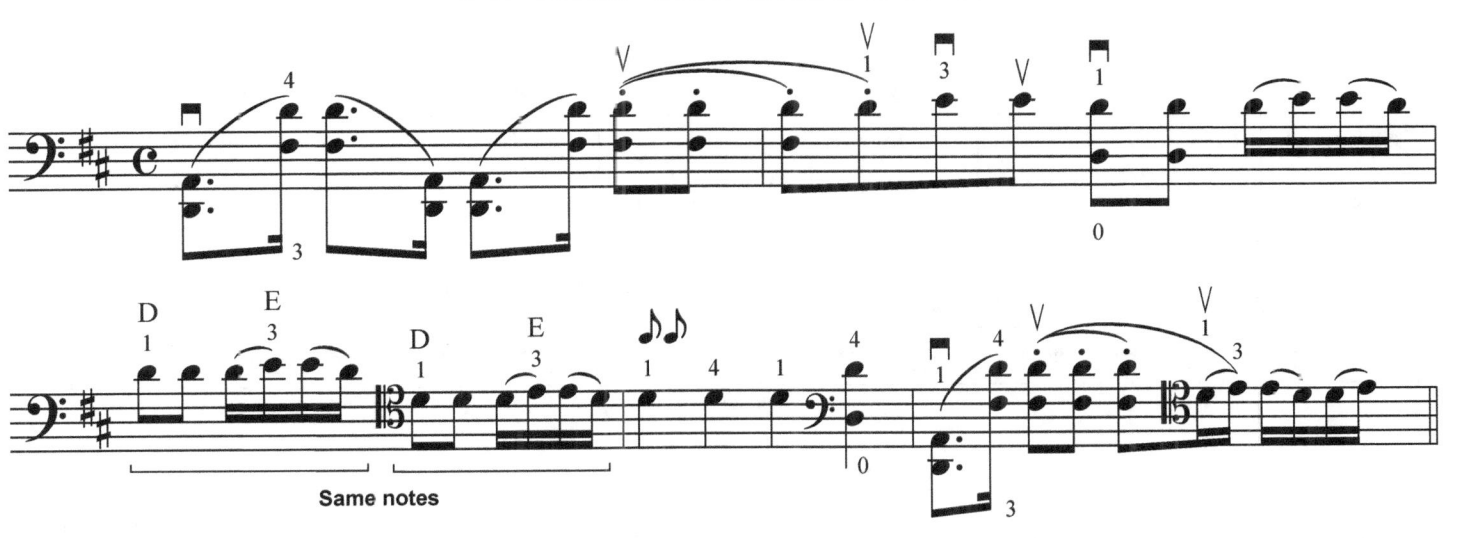

©2020 C. Harvey Publications All Rights Reserved.

36. Shifting and Rhythm: Measures 37-40, 45-48

37. Learning the Notes: Measures 41-44

©2020 C. Harvey Publications   All Rights Reserved.

The Allegro Appassionato Study Book for Cello

38. Learning the Notes: Measures 48-52

39. Agility: Measures 37-52

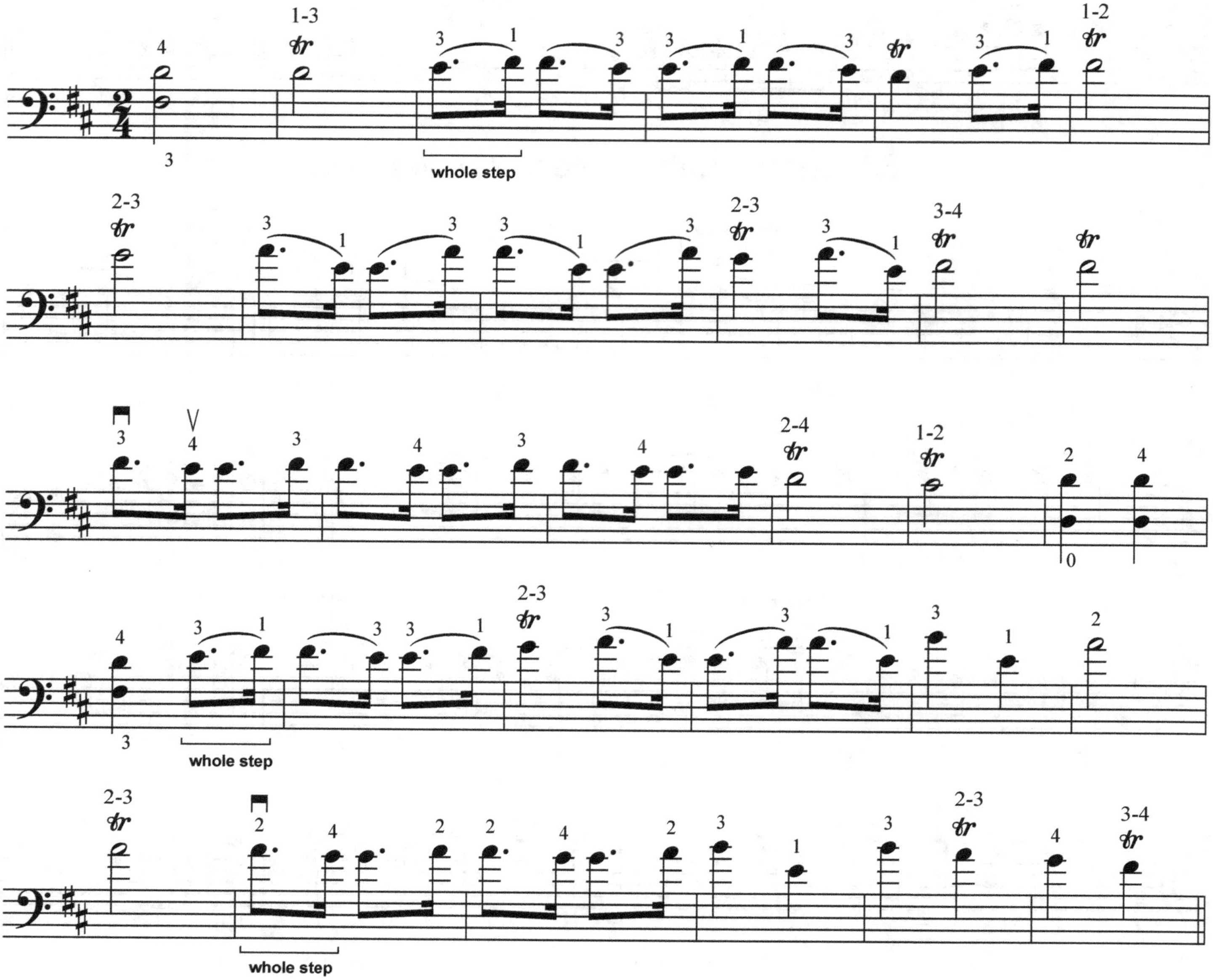

40. Finger Exercise: Measures 37-52

Repeat several times, playing faster each time.

The Allegro Appassionato Study Book for Cello

41. Learning the Notes: Measures 53-56

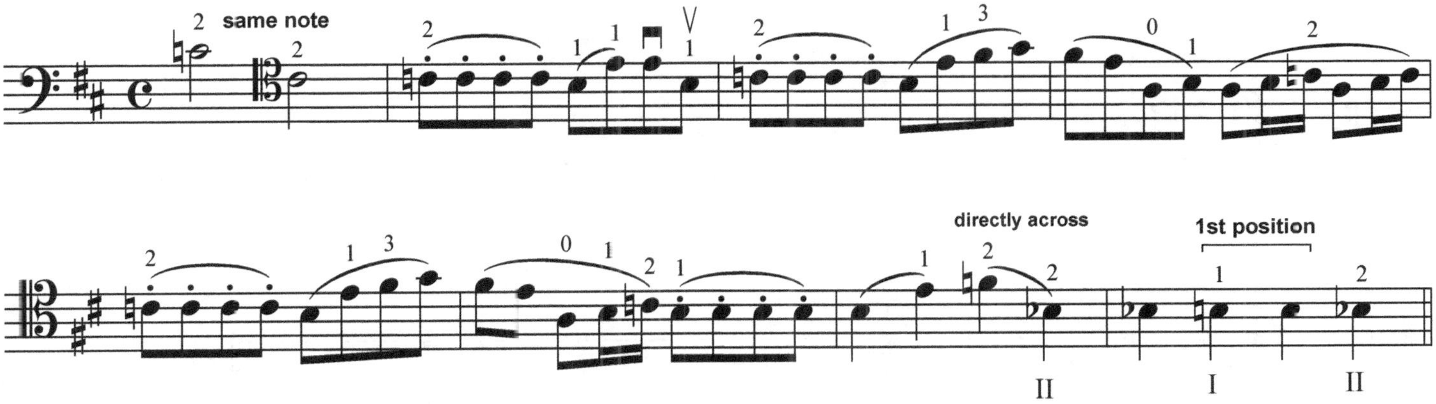

42. Shifting to 6th Position: Measures 58-59

©2020 C. Harvey Publications All Rights Reserved.

26

These next several pages have two distinct bowings. Bowing No. 1 starts the run in M. 62 on an up-bow
and Bowing No. 2 starts the run on a down bow. Play the exercises for whichever bowing you choose to use.

43a. Shifting and Rhythm, Bowing No. 1: Measures 57-61

43b. Shifting and Rhythm, Bowing No. 2: Measures 57-61

44a. Rhythm and Shifting Backwards, Bowing No. 1: Measures 58-61

44b. Rhythm and Shifting Backwards, Bowing No. 2: Measures 58-61

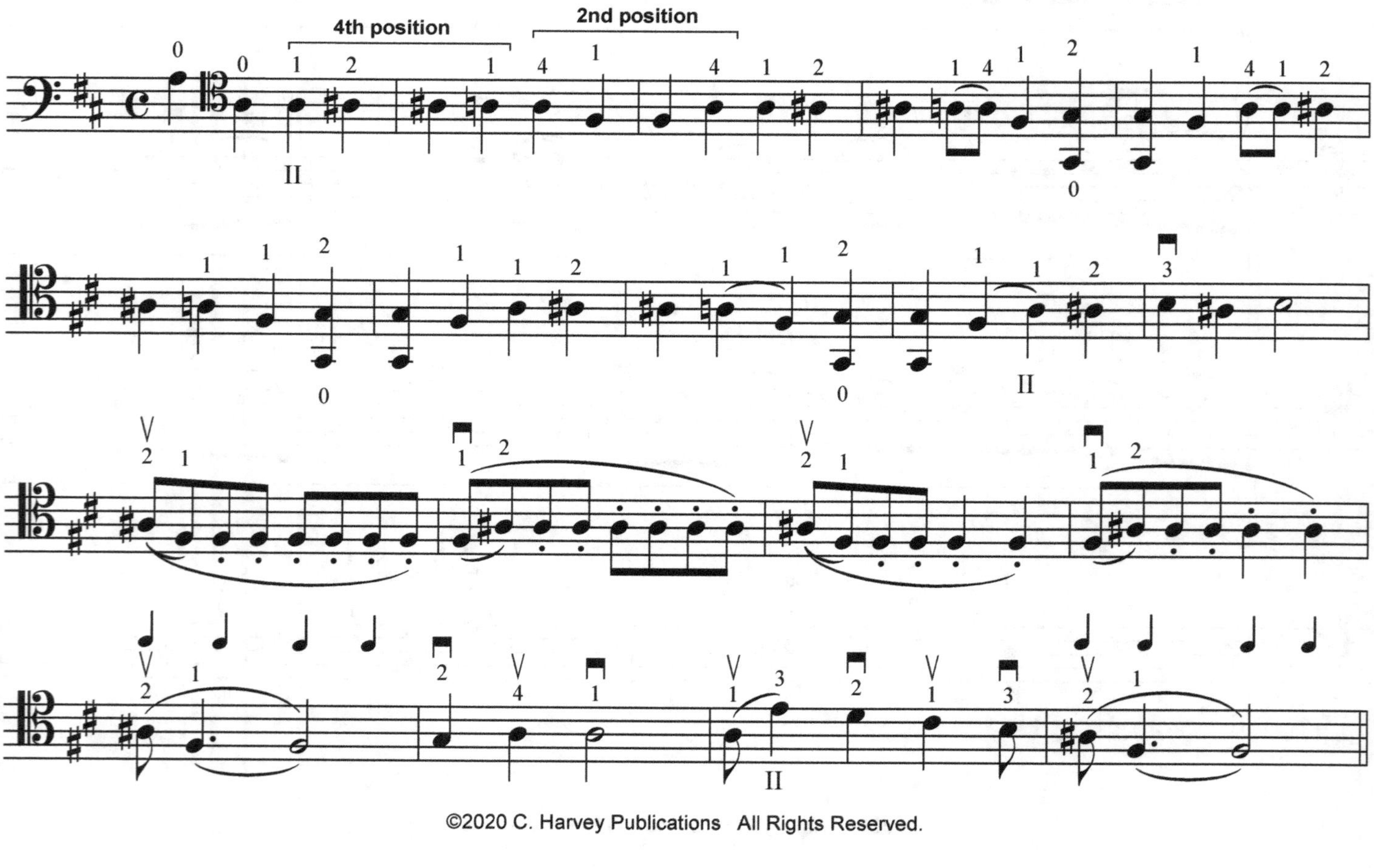

Allegro Appassionato
Section Four: Measures 62-92: Bowing No. 1

Allegro Appassionato
Section Four: Measures 62-92: Bowing No. 2

The Allegro Appassionato Study Book for Cello   31

45. Learning the Notes: Measures 62-65, 68-71

©2020 C. Harvey Publications All Rights Reserved.

46. Learning the Spaces: Measures 62-65, 68-71

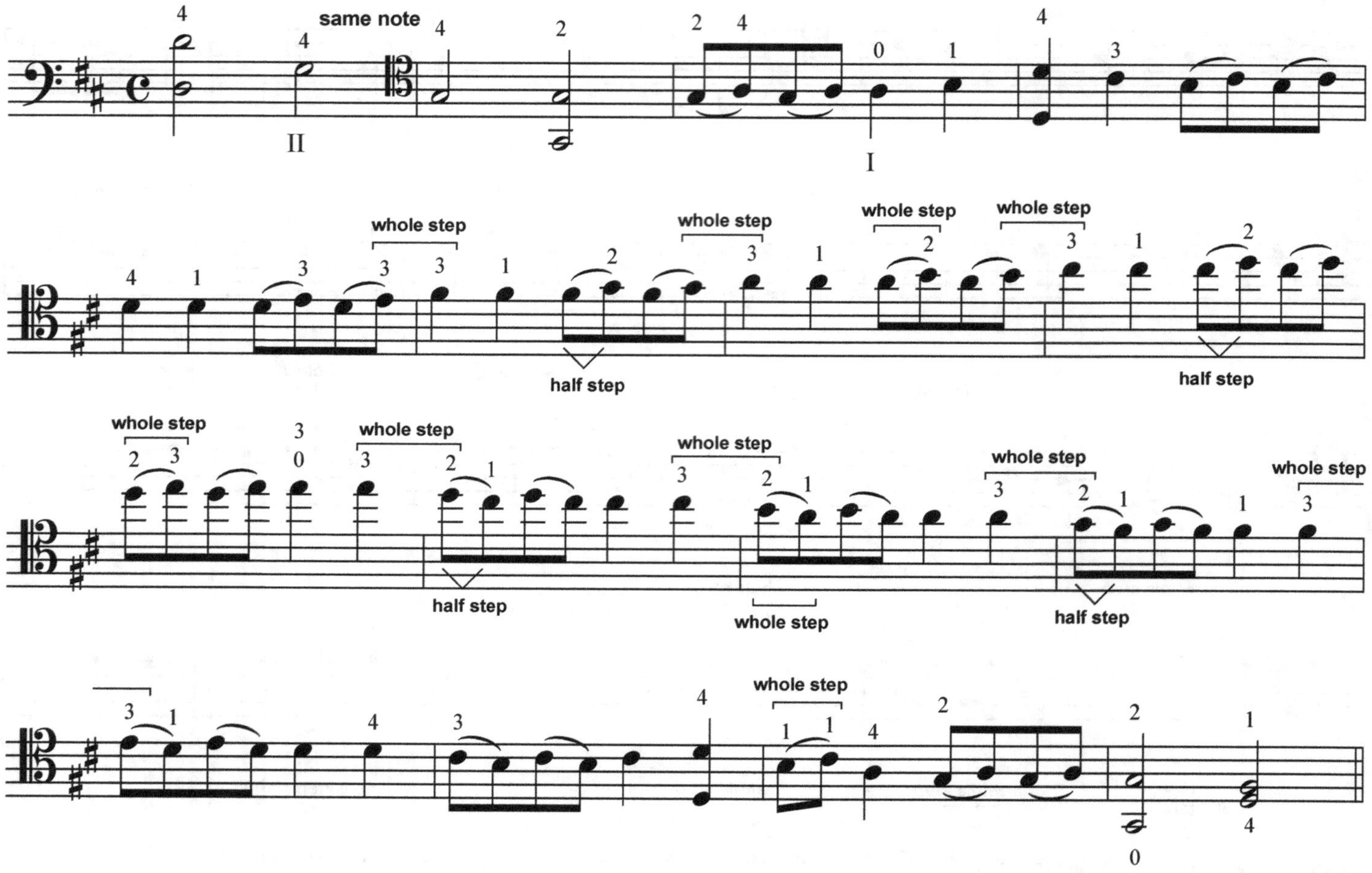

47. Putting the Notes Together In a Scale: Measures 62-65, 68-71

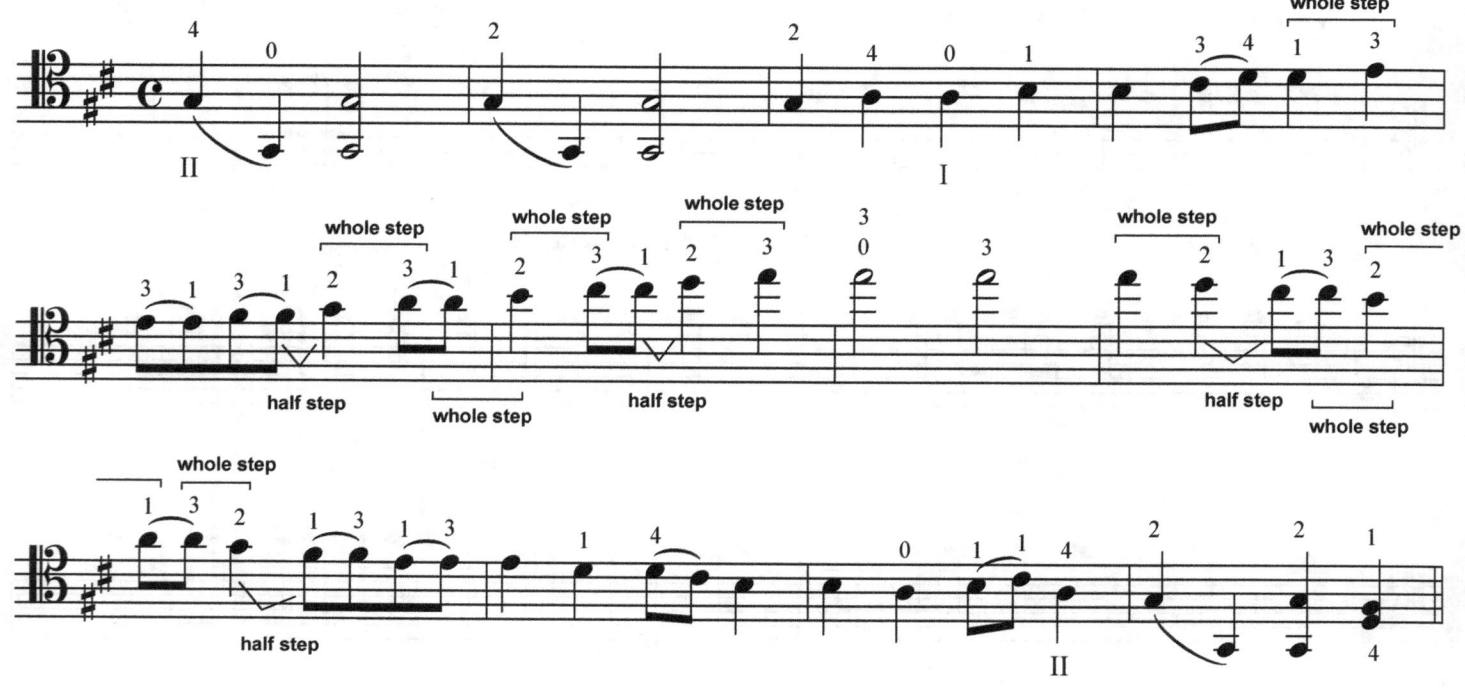

48. Finger Agility and Shifting: Measures 62-65, 68-71

49. Scale and Variations: Measures 62-65, 68-71

35

50. Starting to Add Slurs: Measures 62-65, 68-71

51. Chain of Notes: Measures 62-65, 68-71

©2020 C. Harvey Publications All Rights Reserved.

52. Slur Patterns of 5 Notes: Measures 62-65, 68-71

53a. Staccato to Learn Slurs, Bowing No. 1: Measures 62-65, 68-71

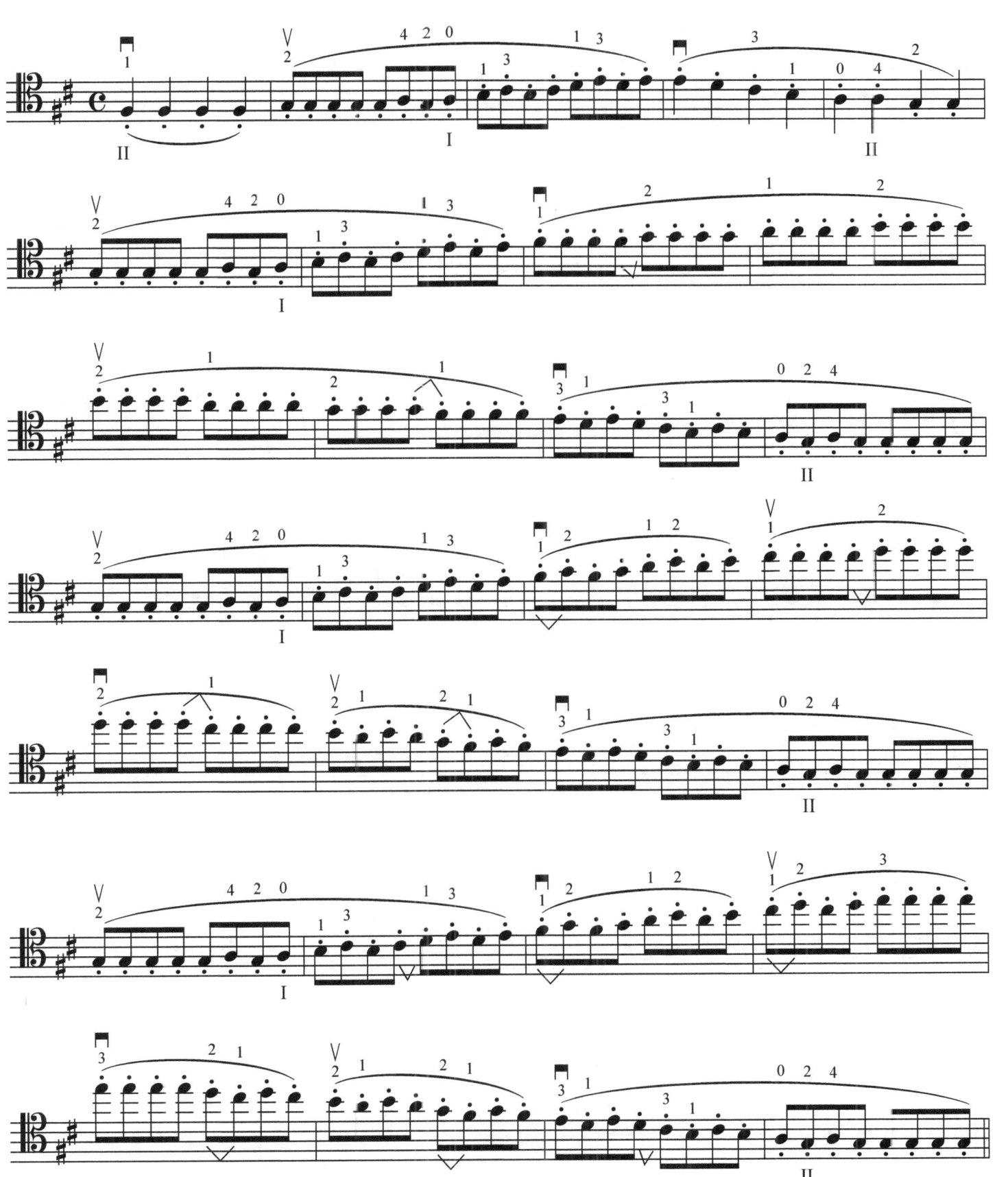

53b. Staccato to Learn Slurs, Bowing No. 2: Measures 62-65, 68-71

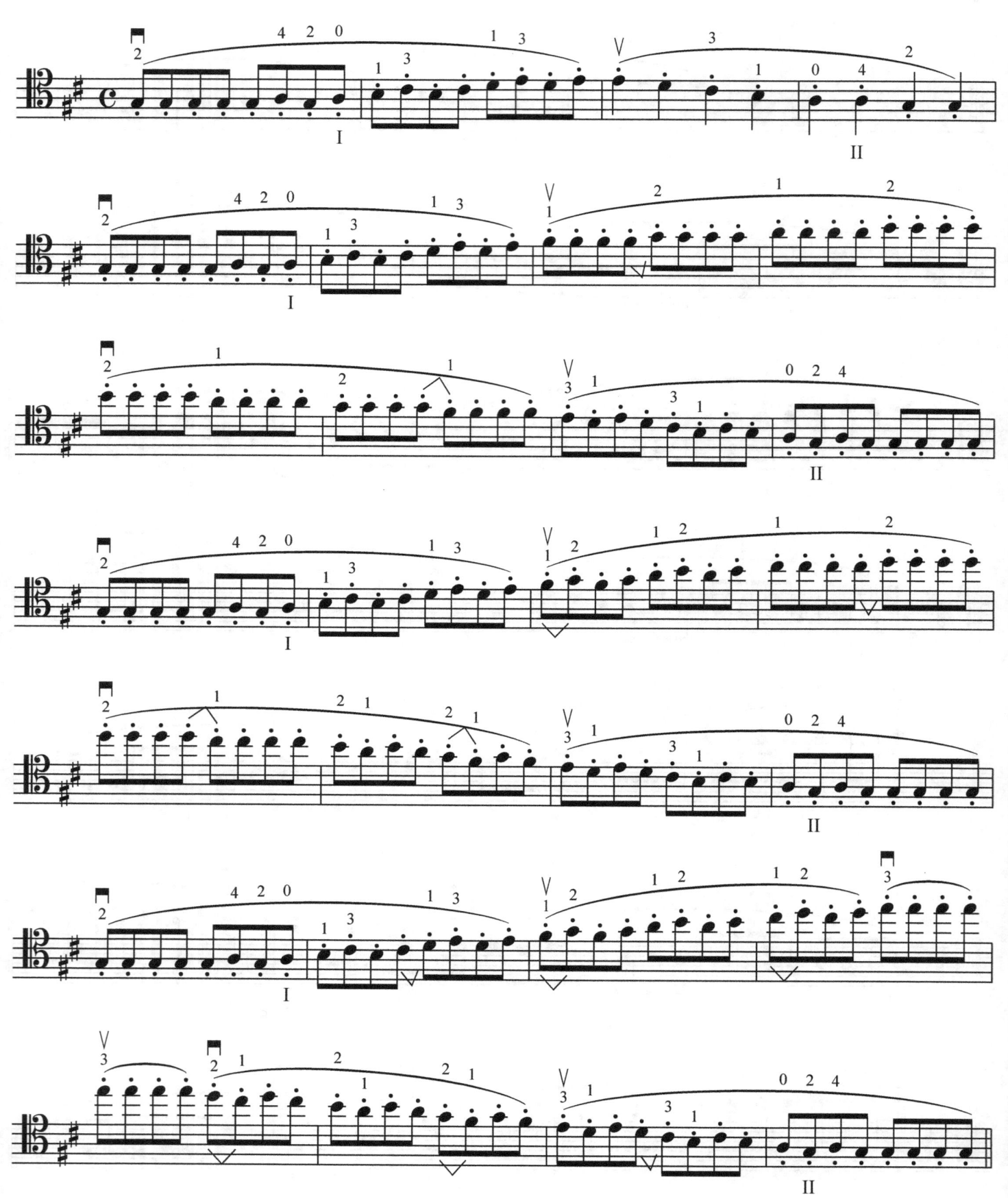

The Allegro Appassionato Study Book for Cello

54a. Building the Slur Patterns, Bowing No. 1: Measures 62-65, 68-71

54b. Building the Slur Patterns, Bowing No. 2: Measures 62-65, 68-71

The Allegro Appassionato Study Book for Cello   41

55. Shifting Back to Half Position (Both Bowings): Measures 62-65, 68-72

56. Trills for Agility (Both Bowings): Measures 62-65, 68-72

©2020 C. Harvey Publications All Rights Reserved.

57. First Speed Exercise (Either Bowing): Measures 62-65, 68-72

58. Second Speed Exercise (Either Bowing): Measures 62-65, 68-72

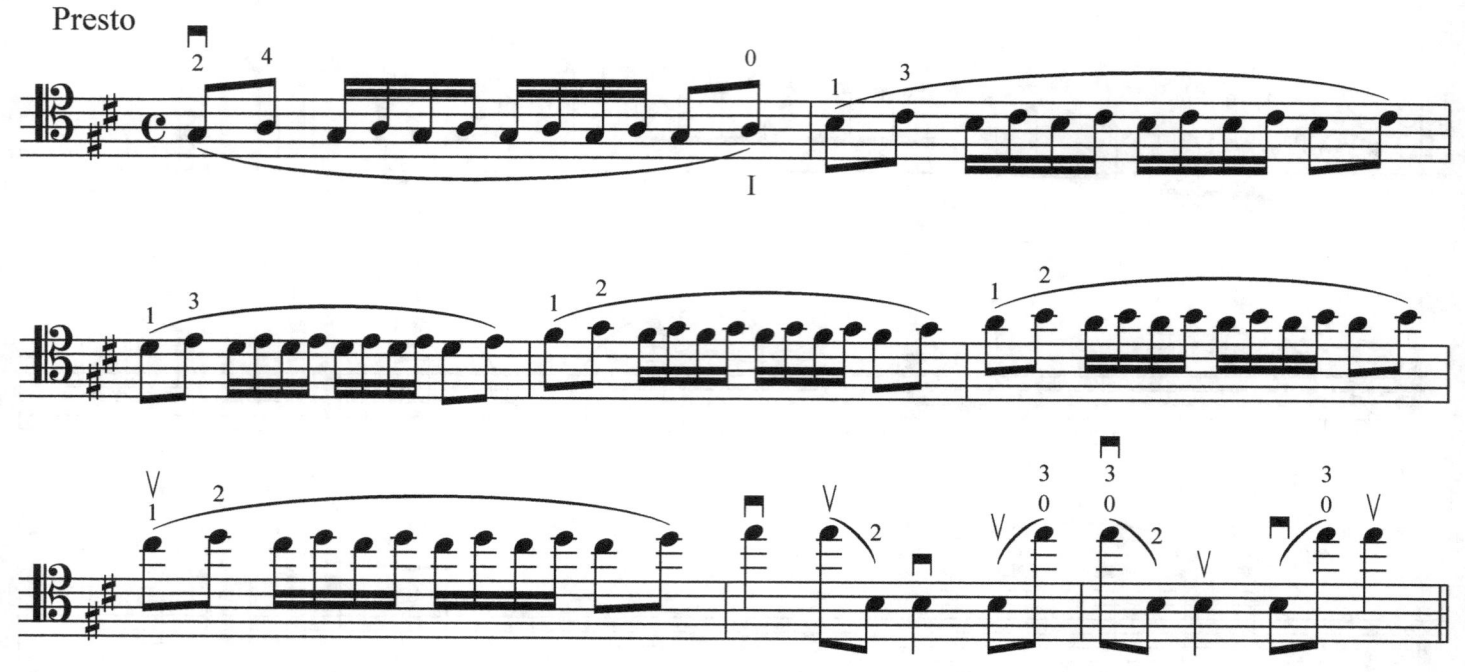

©2020 C. Harvey Publications   All Rights Reserved.

The Allegro Appassionato Study Book for Cello   43

59. Third Speed Exercise (Either Bowing): Measures 62-65, 68-72

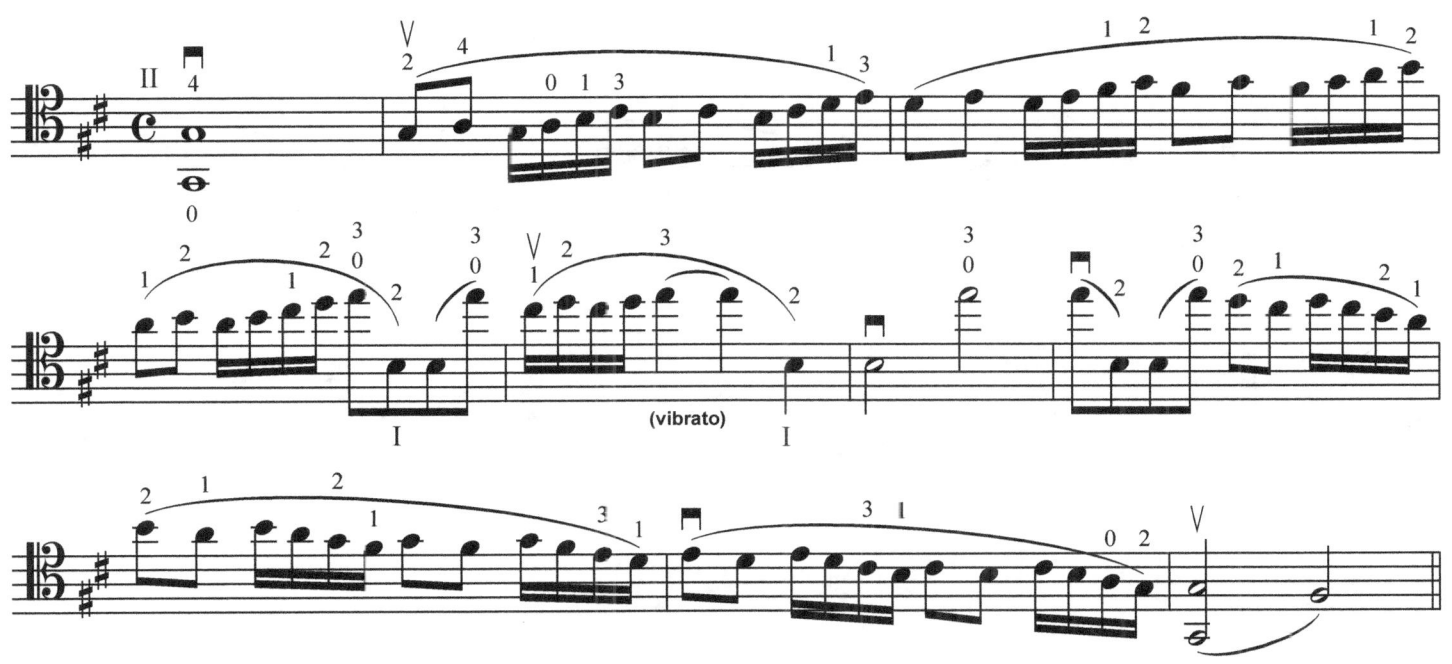

60a. Fourth Speed Exercise, Bowing No.1: Measures 62-65, 68-72

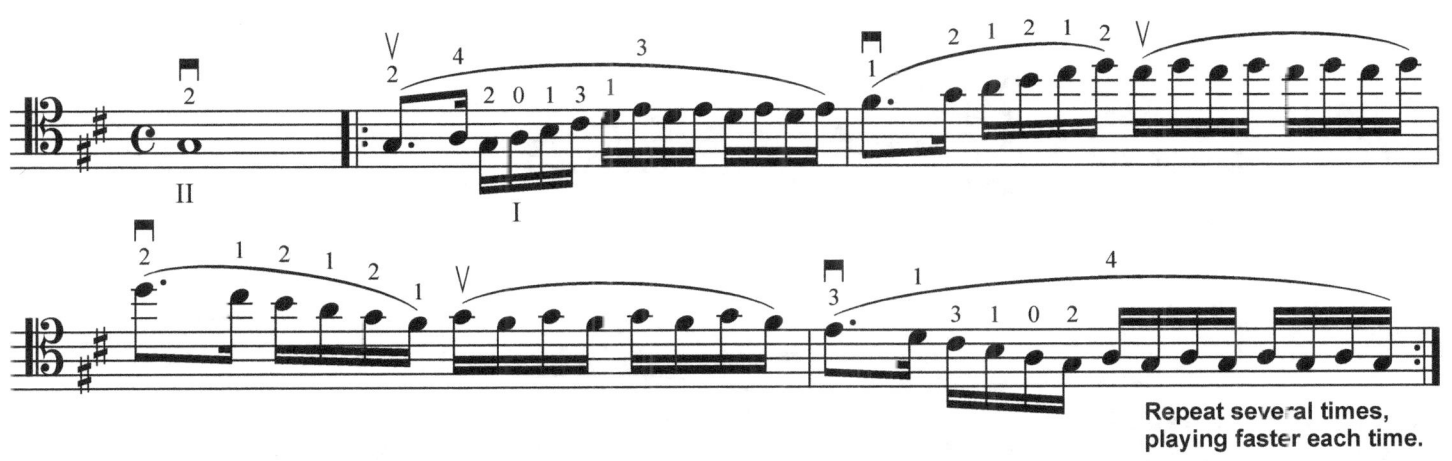

Repeat several times, playing faster each time.

60b. Fourth Speed Exercise, Bowing No.2: Measures 62-65, 68-72

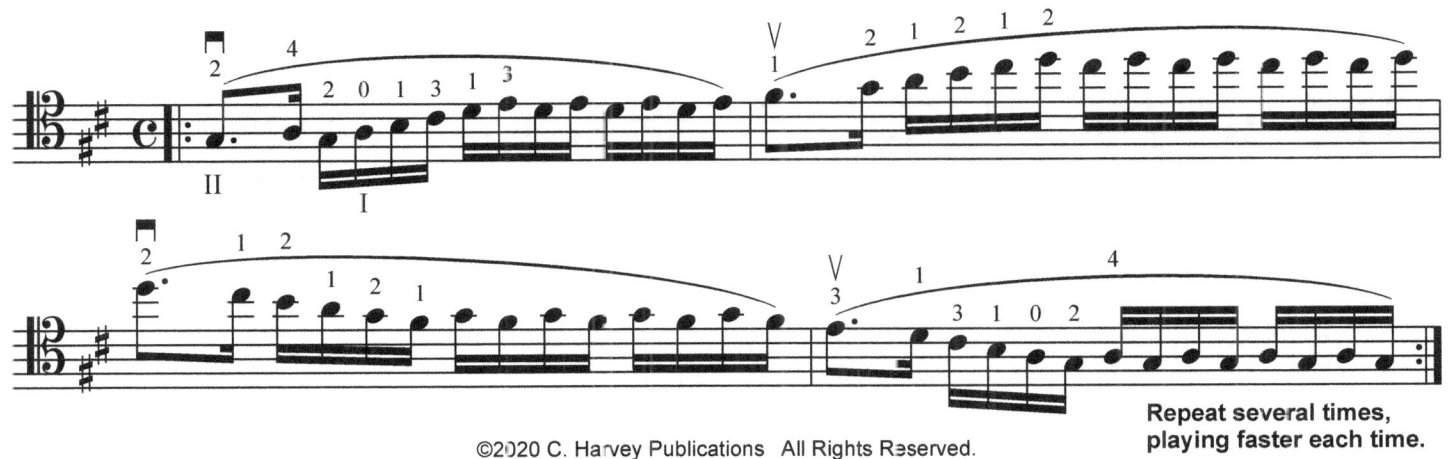

Repeat several times, playing faster each time.

©2020 C. Harvey Publications All Rights Reserved.

61a. Rhythm and Fluency, Bowing No. 1: Measures 60-75

61b. Rhythm and Fluency, Bowing No.2: Measures 62-75

62. Learning the Notes: Measures 73-84

63. Rhythm and Fluency: Measures 73-81

The Allegro Appassionato Study Book for Cello 47

Note: Please see pages 4-13 for work on measures 85-92.

©2020 C. Harvey Publications All Rights Reserved.

Allegro Appassionato
Section Five: Measures 93-116

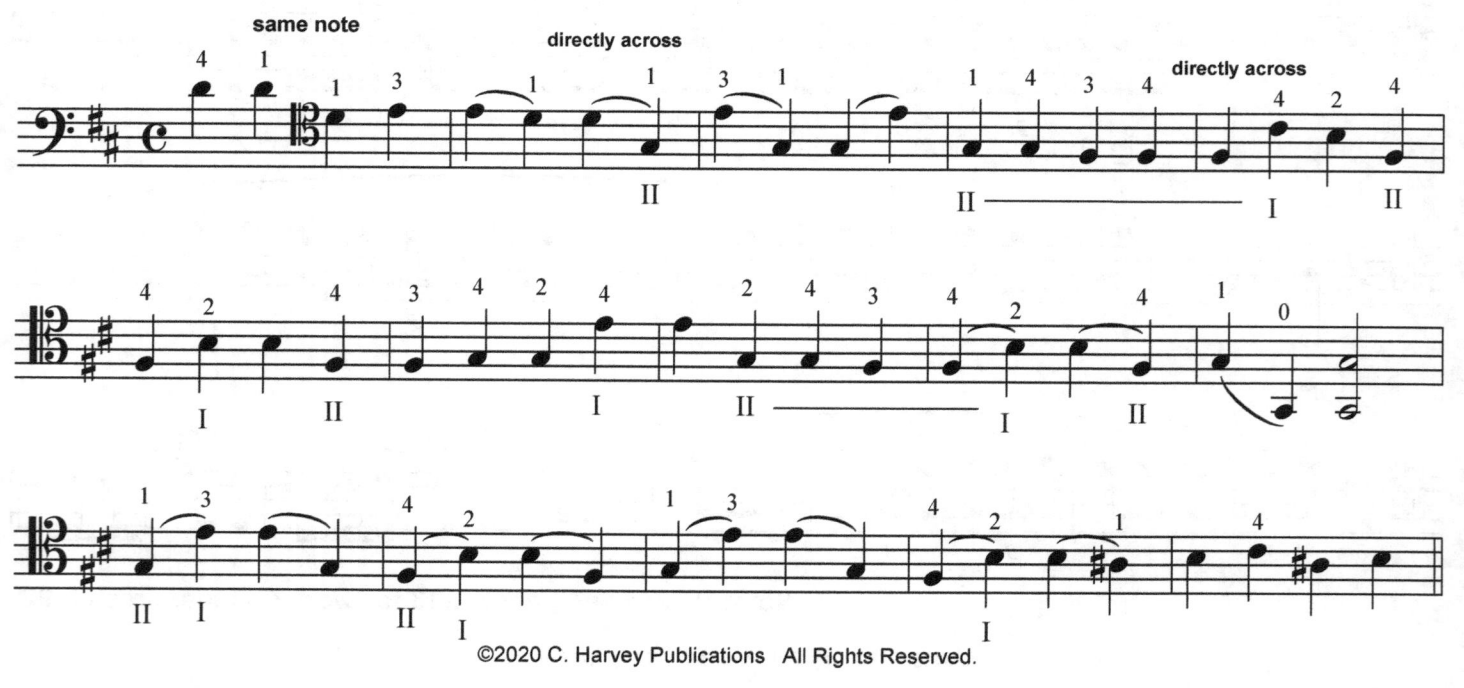

65. Learning the Notes: Measures 93-94

The Allegro Appassionato Study Book for Cello

66. Shifting I: Measures 95-96

67. Shifting II: Measures 96-98

©2020 C. Harvey Publications All Rights Reserved.

68. Learning the Notes: Measures 93-116

The Allegro Appassionato Study Book for Cello   51

69. Rhythm and Fluency: Measures 93-116

Allegro Appassionato
Section Six: Measures 117-133

70. Double Stops: Measures 117-118, 15-126

71. Rhythm and Fluency: Measures 93-116

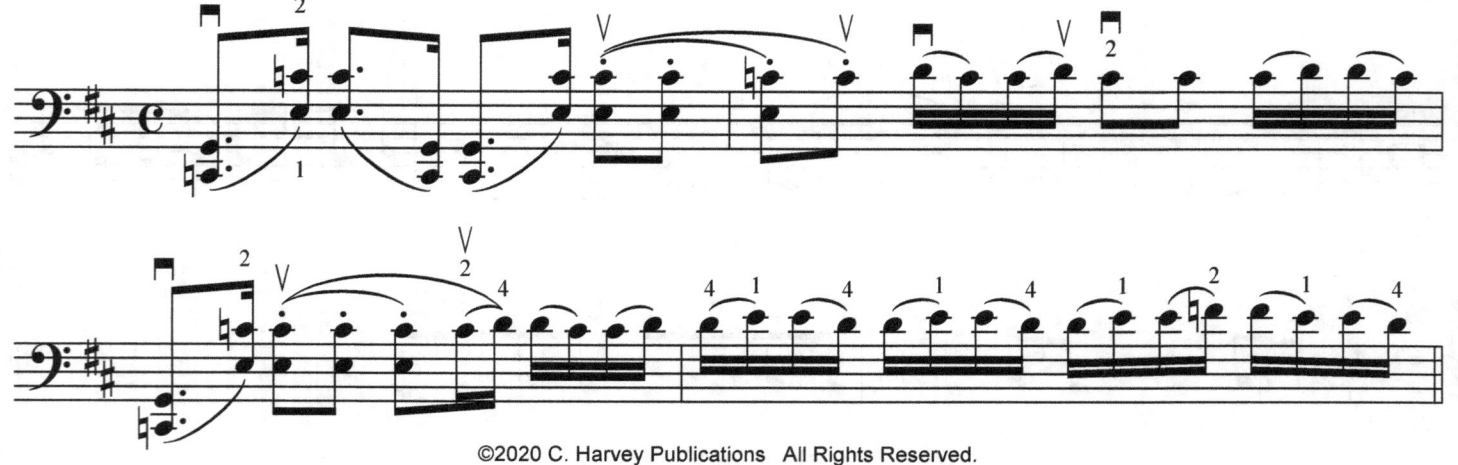

The Allegro Appassionato Study Book for Cello

72. Learning the Notes: Measures 117-129

73. Shifting: Measures 128-133

Allegro Appassionato
Section Seven: Measures 134-156

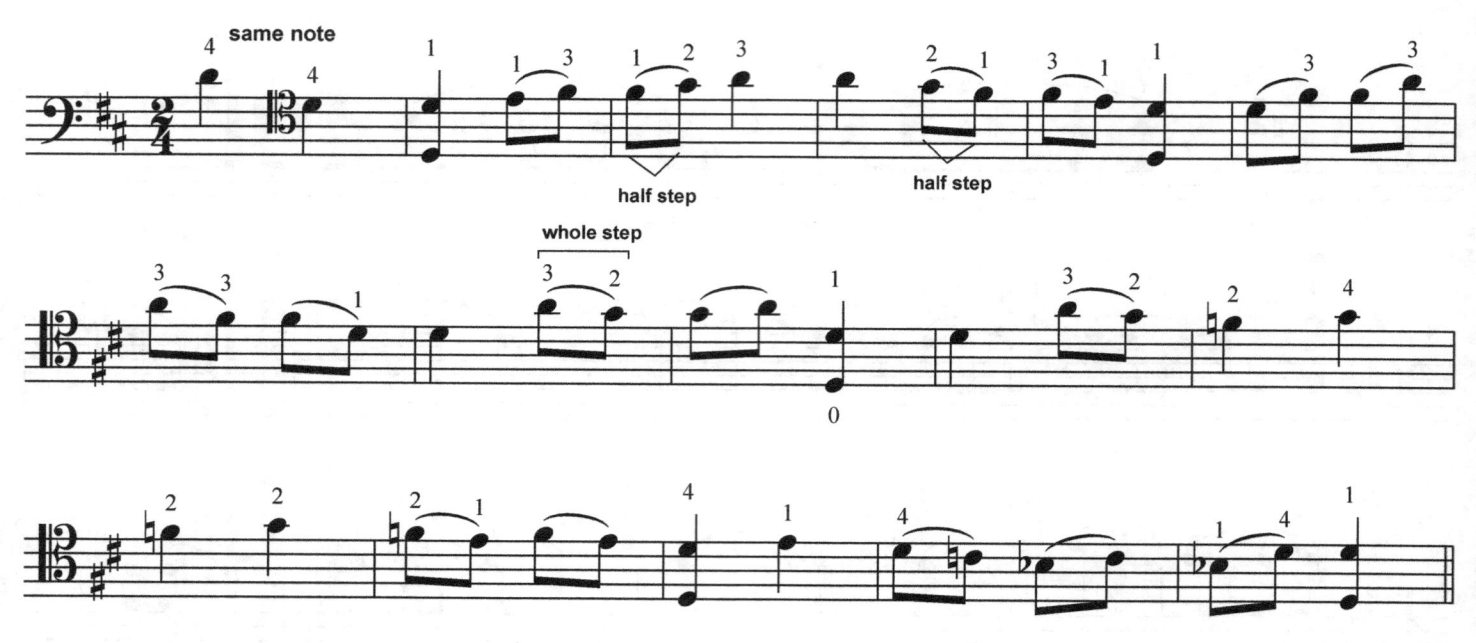

The Allegro Appassionato Study Book for Cello

74. Shifting: Measures 133-144

75. Rhythm: Measures 136-146

The Allegro Appassionato Study Book for Cello
57

76. Learning the Notes Across Strings: Measures 146-153

77. Shifting Back Into the Next Section: Measure 146

©2020 C. Harvey Publications All Rights Reserved.

78. Shifting Through the Positions: Measures 146-153

79. Bowing Study No. 1: Measures 146-153

80. Bowing Study No. 2: Measures 146-153

81. Bowing Study No. 3: Measures 146-153

82. Putting the Section Together: Measures 146-153

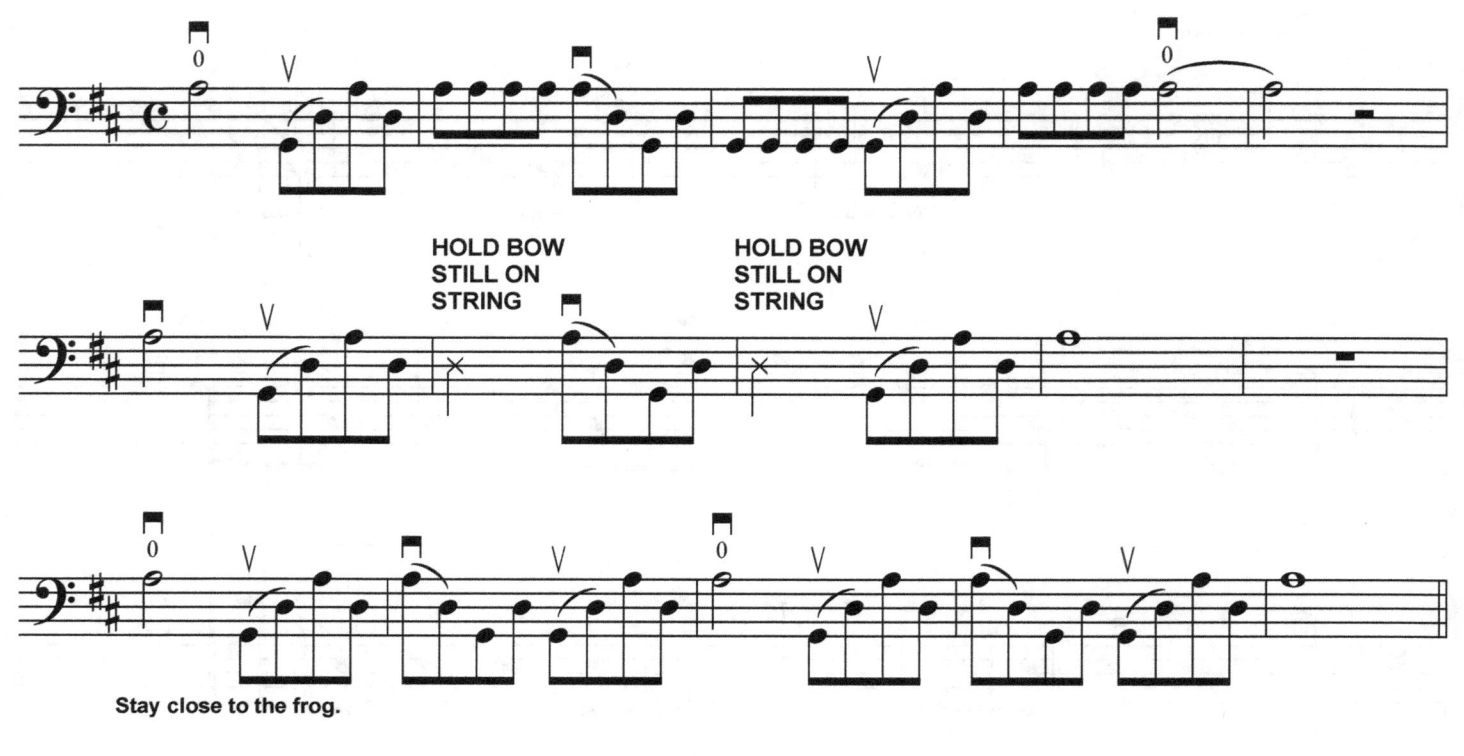

83. Shifting I: Measures 153-156

84. Shifting II: Measures 153-156

85. Agility I: Measures 153-164

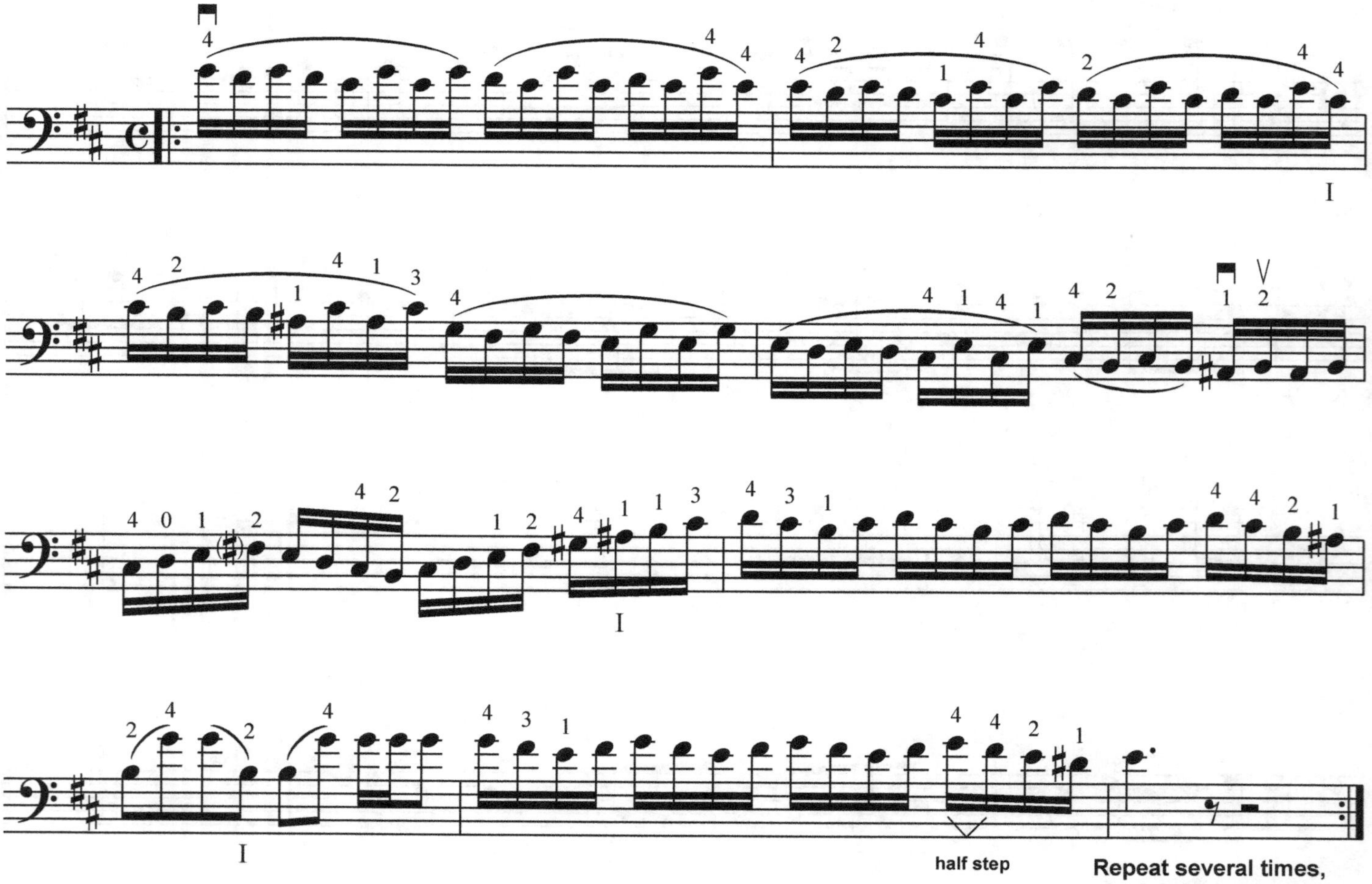

half step

Repeat several times, playing faster each time.

The Allegro Appassionato Study Book for Cello
63

86. Agility II: Measures 153-164

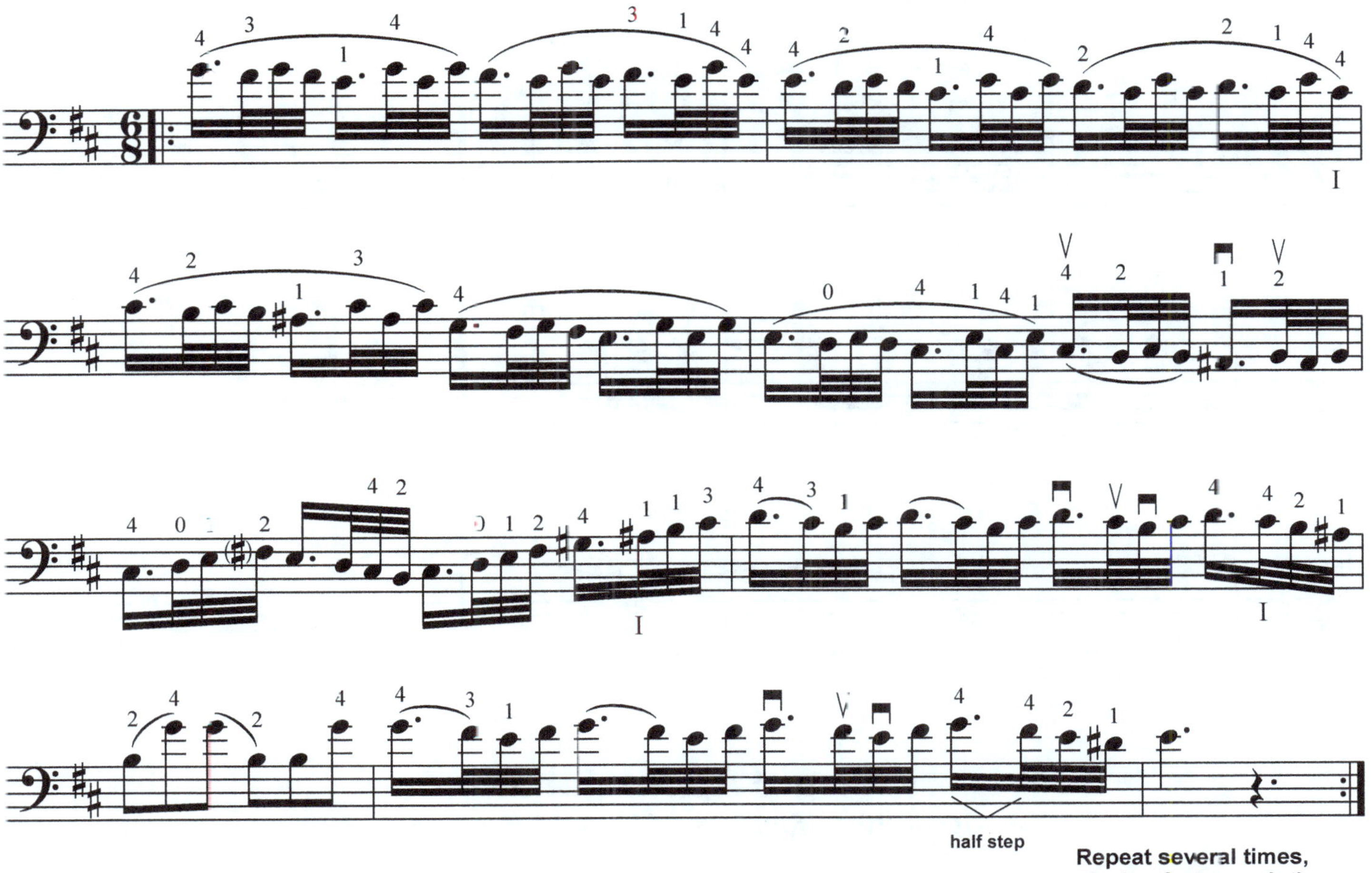

half step

Repeat several times, playing faster each time.

87. Agility III: Measures 153-156

©2020 C. Harvey Publications All Rights Reserved.

Allegro Appassionato
Section Eight: Measures 157-168: Bowing No. 1

Allegro Appassionato
Section Eight: Measures 157-168: Bowing No. 2

As the measures in this section are repeated from the beginning of the piece, exercises for these measures are found on pp. 4-16.

Allegro Appassionato
Section Nine: Measures 169-183: Bowing No. 1

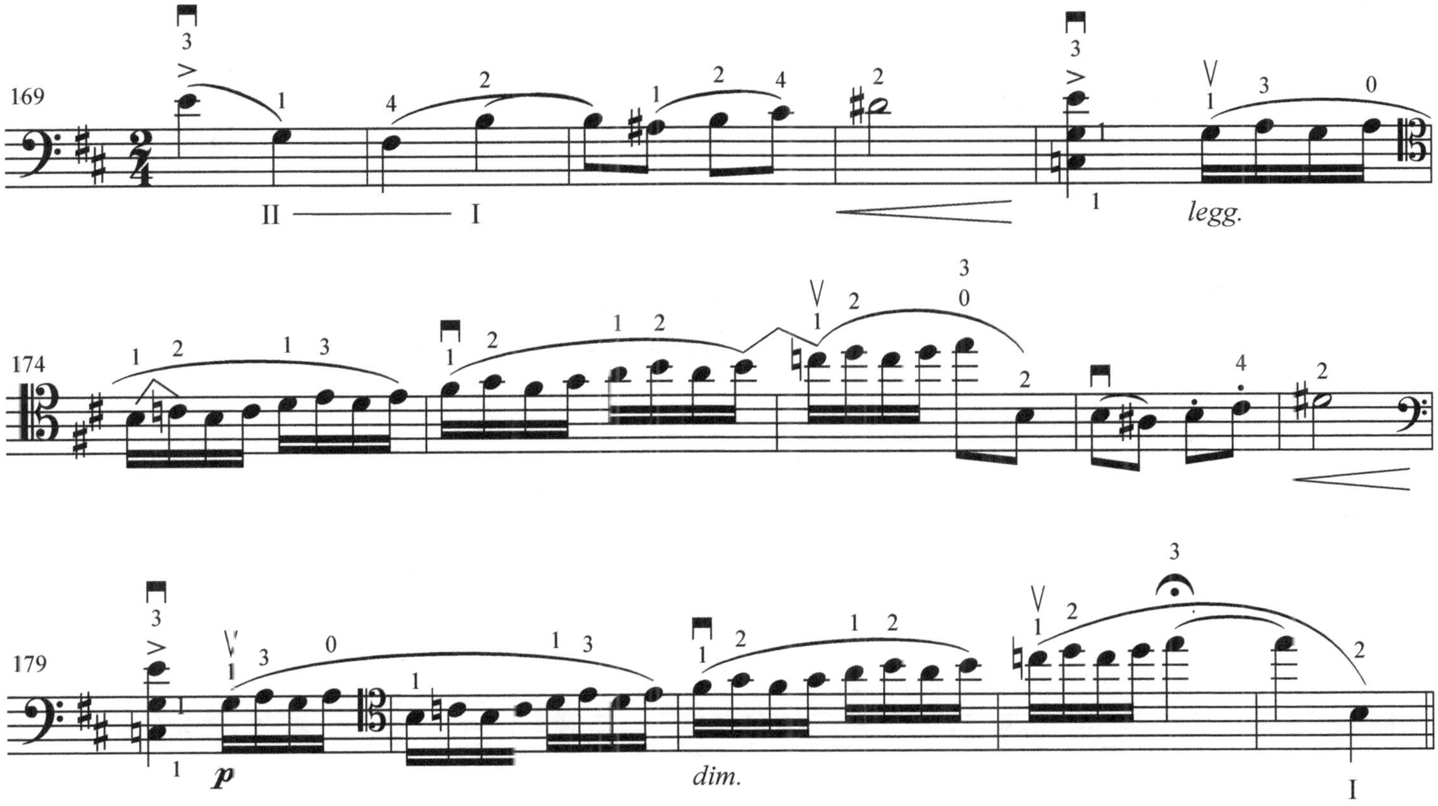

Allegro Appassionato
Section Nine: Measures 169-183: Bowing No. 2

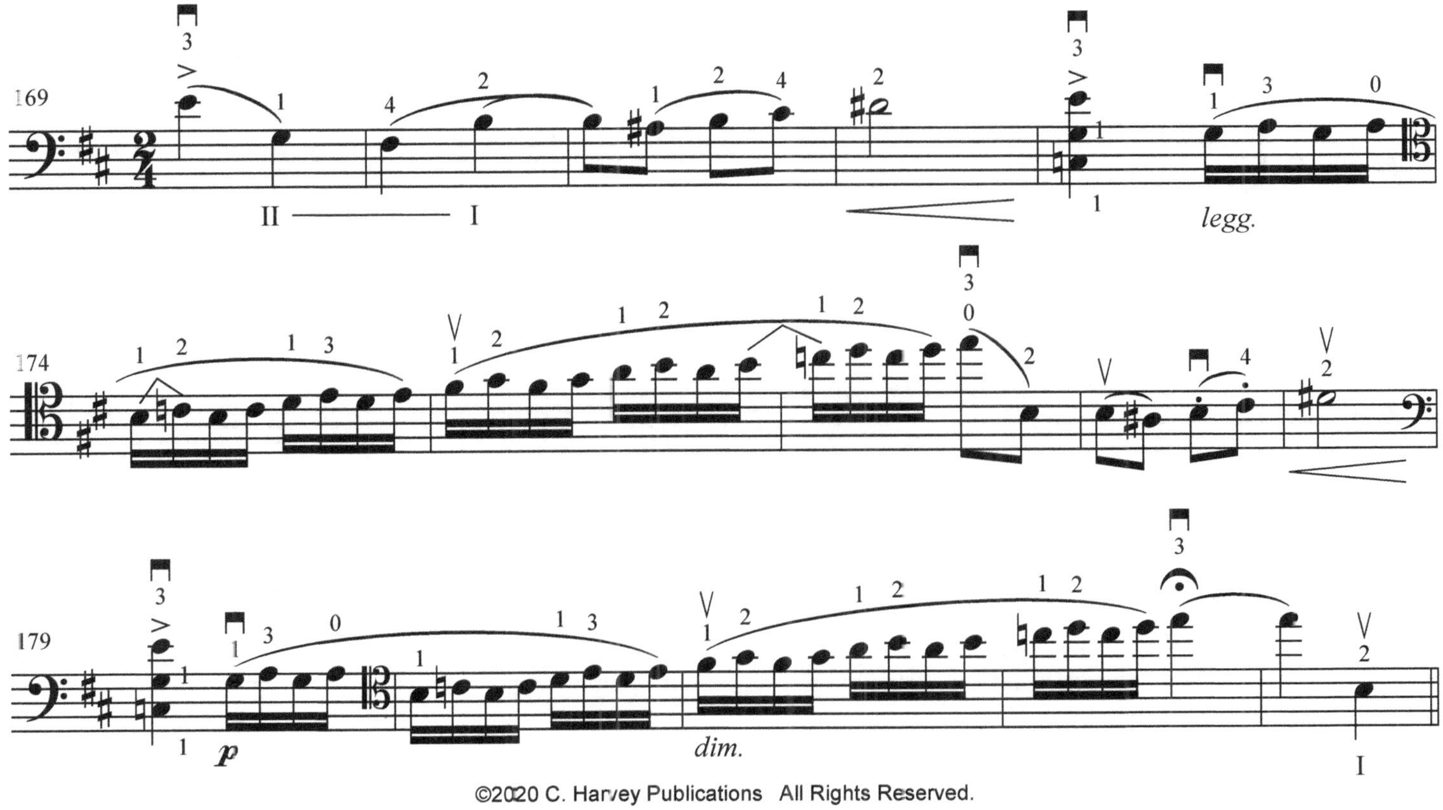

88. Learning the Notes: Measures 169-173 (Both Bowings)

89. Shifting: Measures 173-183

The Allegro Appassionato Study Book for Cello

90. Learning the Spaces: Measures 173-183

91. Putting the Notes Together in a Scale: Measures 173-183

©2020 C. Harvey Publications All Rights Reserved.

92. Finger Agility and Shifting: Measures 173-183

93. Scale and Variations: Measures 173-183

The Allegro Appassionato Study Book for Cello   71

94. Starting to Add Slurs: Measures 173-183

95. Chain of Notes: Measures 173-183

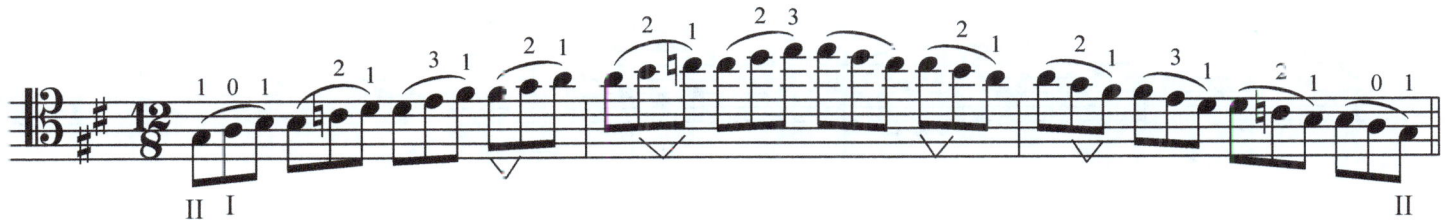

©2020 C. Harvey Publications   All Rights Reserved.

96. Slur Patterns of Five Notes: Measures 173-183

The Allegro Appassionato Study Book for Cello

97a. Staccato to Learn Slurs, Bowing No. 1: Measures 173-183

©2020 C. Harvey Publications All Rights Reserved.

97b. Staccato to Learn Slurs, Bowing No. 2: Measures 173-183

The Allegro Appassionato Study Book for Cello

98a. Building the Slur Patterns, Bowing No. 1: Measures 173-183

98b. Building the Slur Patterns, Bowing No. 2: Measures 173-183

©2020 C. Harvey Publications All Rights Reserved.

The Allegro Appassionato Study Book for Cello
77

99. Shifting Back to Half Position (Both Bowings): Measures 173-183

100. Trills for Agility (Both Bowings): Measures 173-183

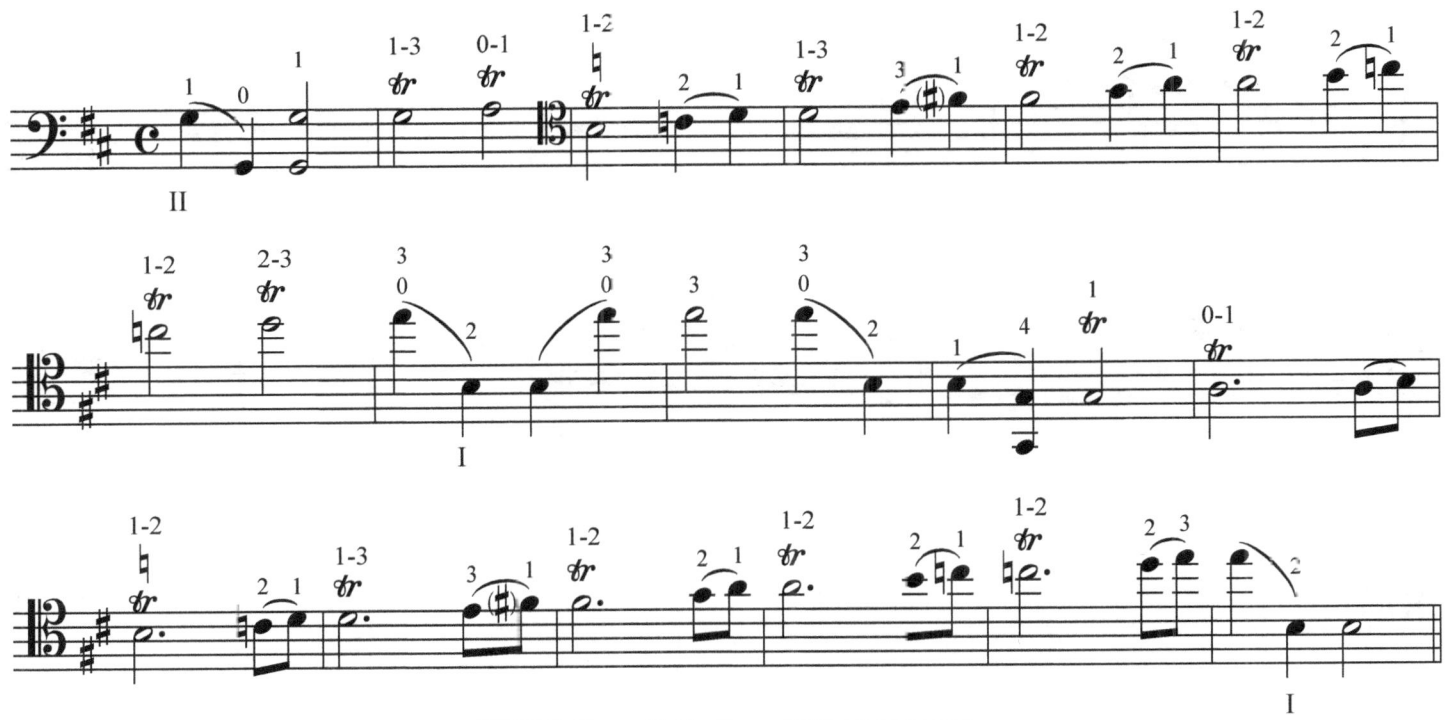

©2020 C. Harvey Publications All Rights Reserved.

101. First Speed Exercise (Both Bowings): Measures 173-183

102. Second Speed Exercise (Both Bowings): Measures 173-183

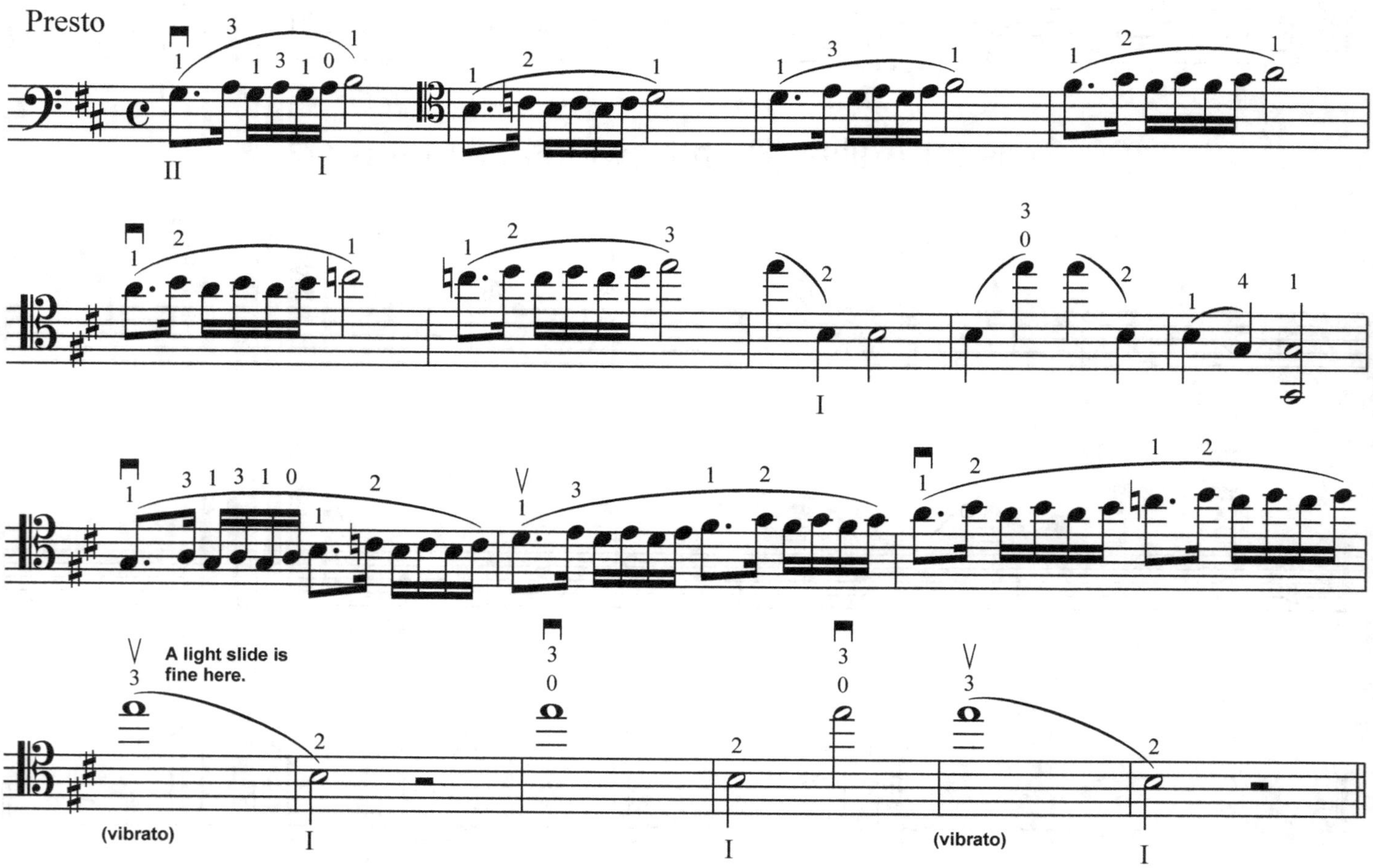

103. Third Speed Exercise (Both Bowings): Measures 173-183

104a. Fourth Speed Exercise, Bowing No. 1: Measures 173-183

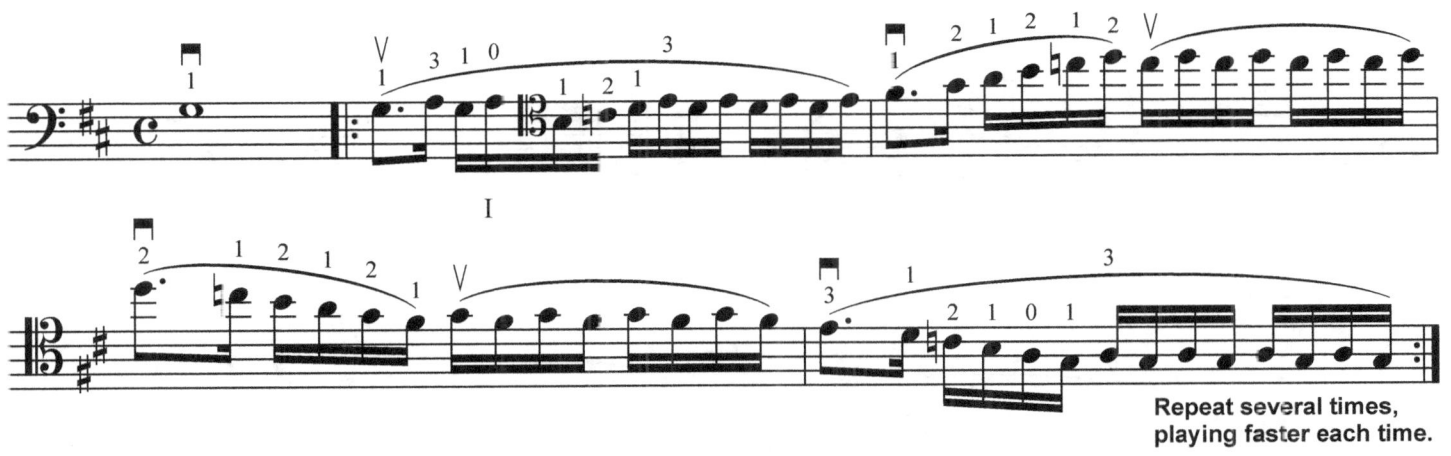

Repeat several times, playing faster each time.

104b. Fourth Speed Exercise, Bowing No. 2: Measures 173-183

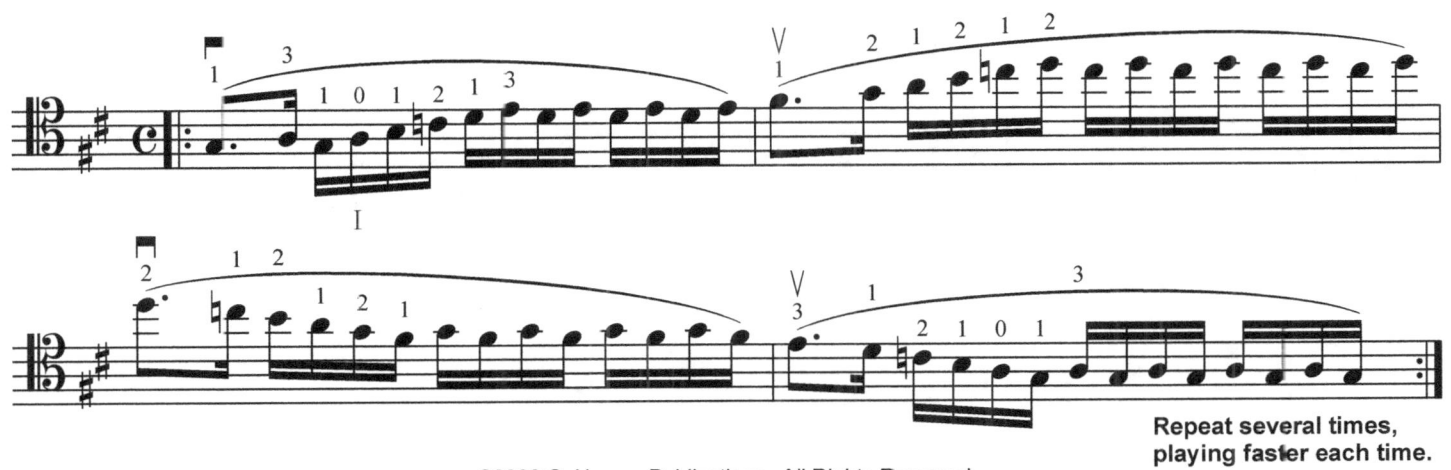

Repeat several times, playing faster each time.

©2020 C. Harvey Publications All Rights Reserved.

105a. Rhythm and Fluency, Bowing No. 1: Measures 173-183

105b. Rhythm and Fluency, Bowing No. 2: Measures 173-183

Allegro Appassionato
Section Ten: Measures 184-215 (end)

Note: See p. 46 for more work on measures 184-188, 192-196

The Allegro Appassionato Study Book for Cello

106. Shifting: Measures 184-195

107. Bowing: Measures 194-202

108. Agility I: Measures 203-208

Repeat several times, playing faster each time.

The Allegro Appassionato Study Book for Cello

109. Agility II: Measures 203-208

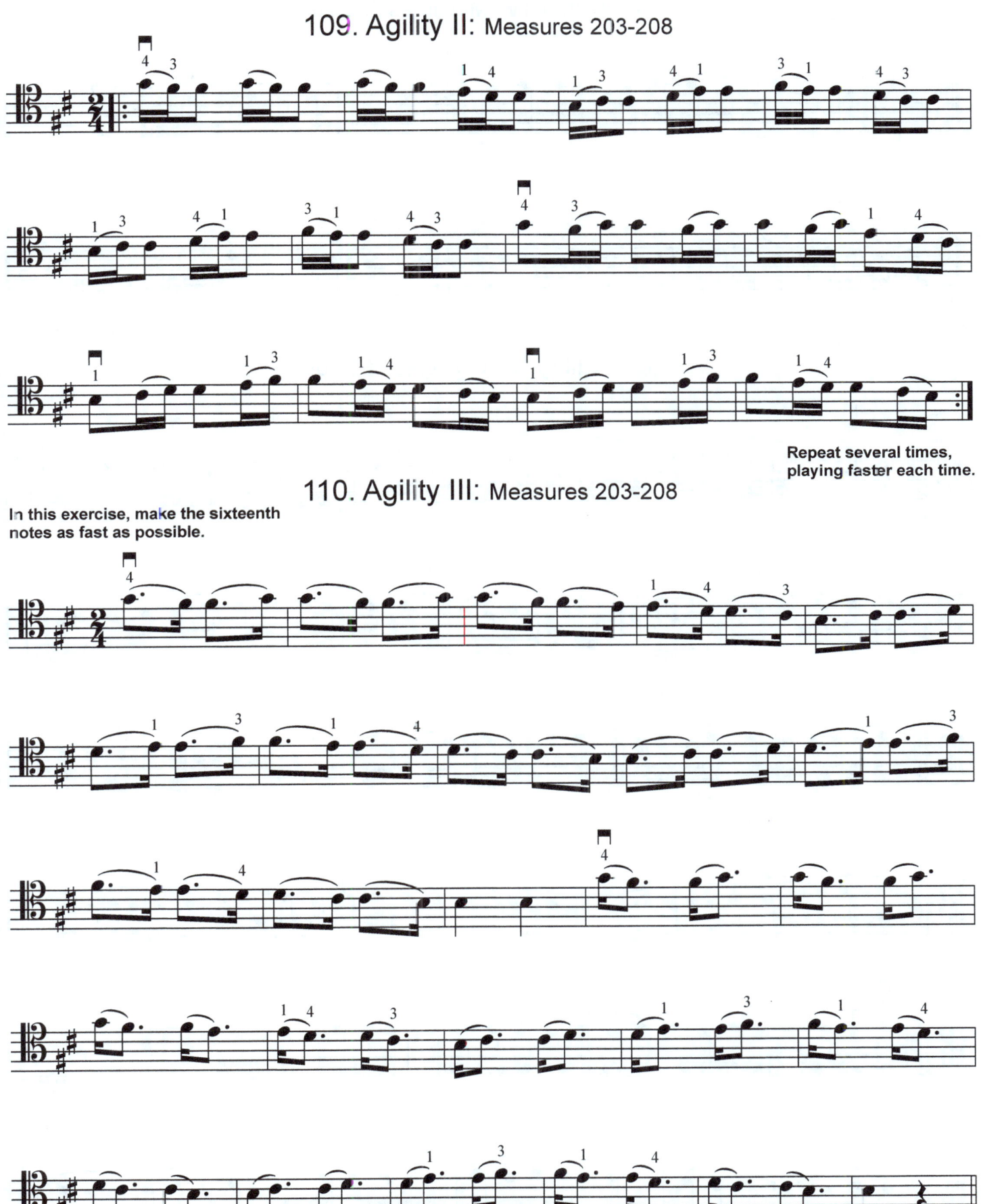

Repeat several times, playing faster each time.

110. Agility III: Measures 203-208

In this exercise, make the sixteenth notes as fast as possible.

111. Agility IV: Measures 203-208

112. Agility V: Measures 203-208

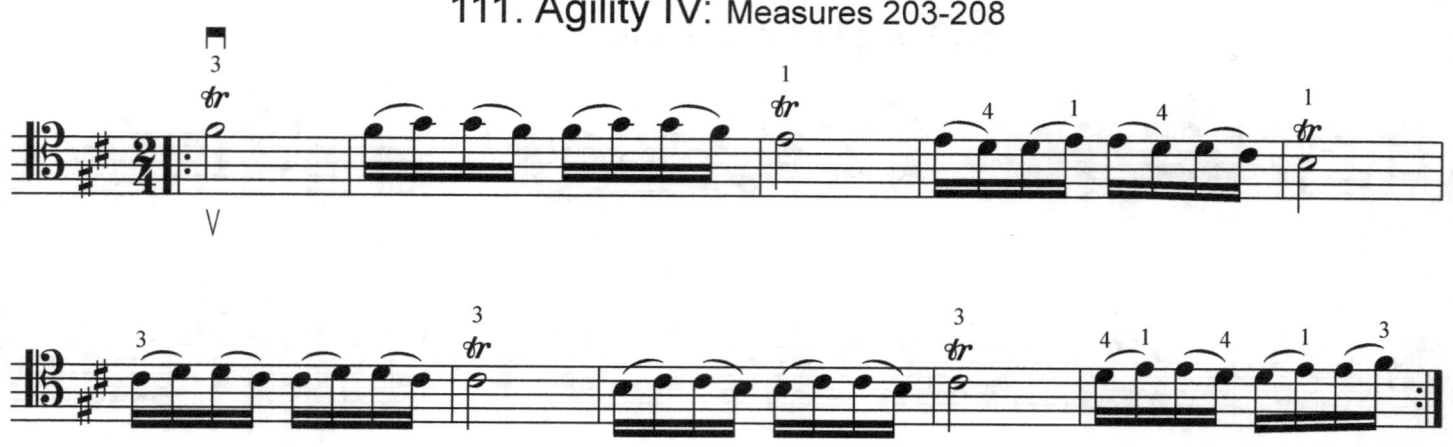

Repeat, starting on an up-bow.

The Allegro Appassionato Study Book for Cello
87

113. Building the Chords: Measures 209-211

©2020 C. Harvey Publications   All Rights Reserved.

114a. Shifting, Top Fingering: Measures 211-214

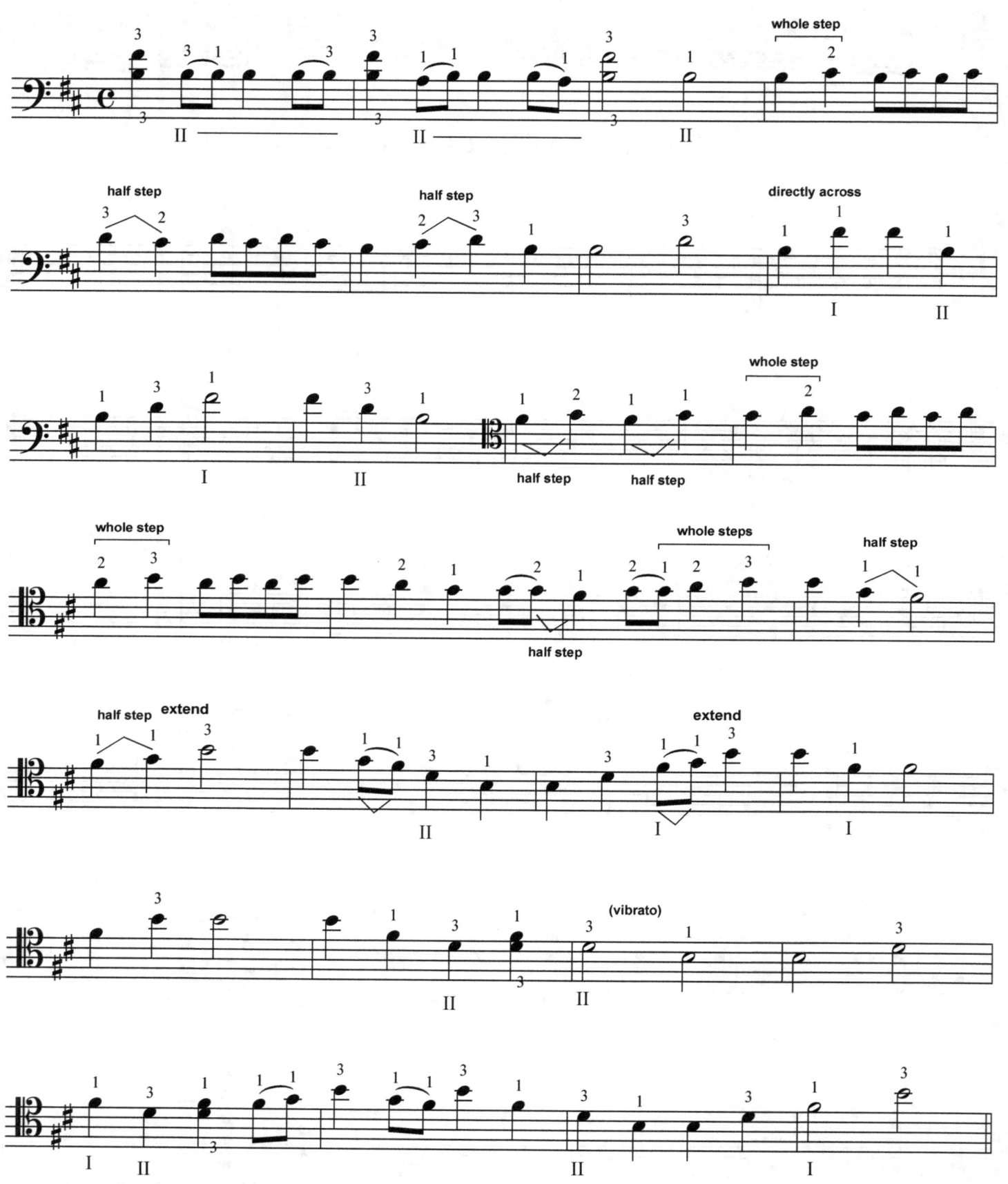

The Allegro Appassionato Study Book for Cello 89

114b. Shifting, Bottom Fingering: Measures 211-214

115. Building the Chord: Measures 213-215

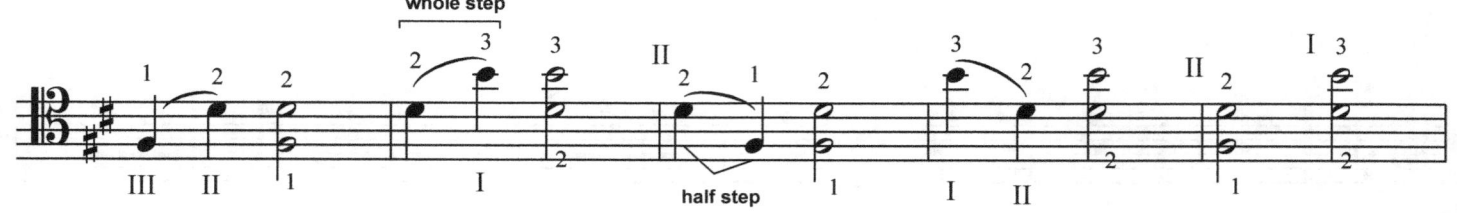

116a. Finding the Chord, Top Fingering: Measures 210-215

©2020 C. Harvey Publications   All Rights Reserved.

The Allegro Appassionato Study Book for Cello

116b. Finding the Chord, Bottom Fingering: Measures 210-215

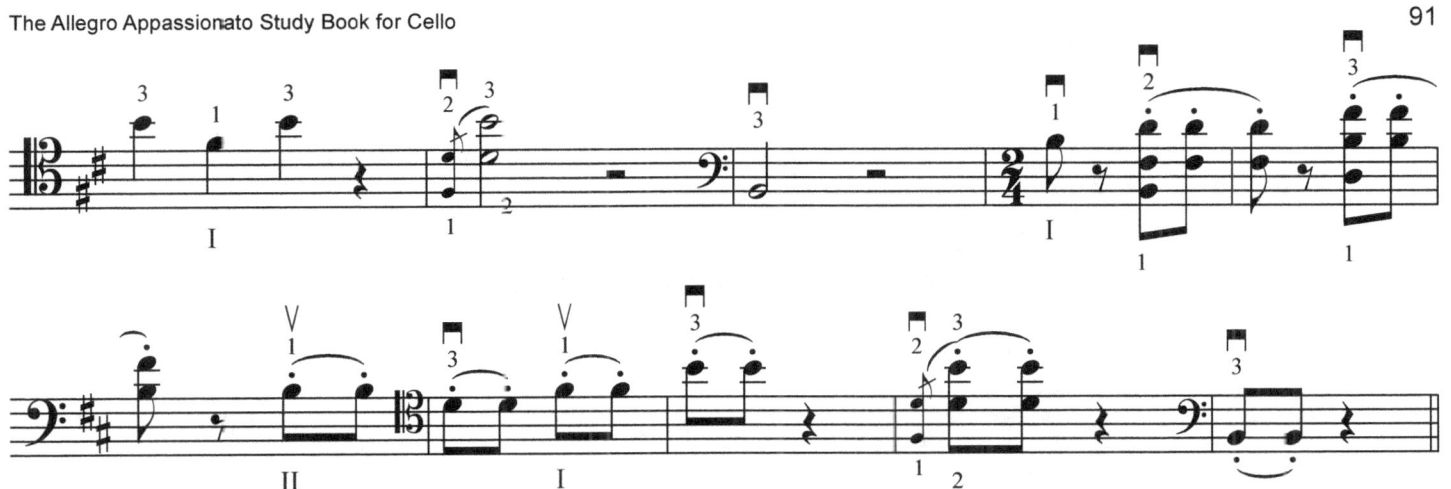

©2020 C. Harvey Publications   All Rights Reserved.

Allegro Appassionato
Bowing No. 1

Camille Saint-Saëns

The Allegro Appassionato Study Book for Cello

The Allegro Appassionato Study Book for Cello

Allegro Appassionato
Bowing No. 2

Camille Saint-Saëns

The Allegro Appassionato Study Book for Cello

The Allegro Appassionato Study Book for Cello

©2020 C. Harvey Publications All Rights Reserved.

The Allegro Appassionato Study Book for Cello

99

available from **www.charveypublications.com**: CHP346
The Swan Study Book for Cello

Note: The Swan is broken up into sections in this study book. The complete Swan is at the back of the book.

The Swan
Section One: Measures 1-5

The Swan, by Camille Saint-Saens
Exercises by Cassia Harvey

Learning the Notes and the First Shift
Measure 1

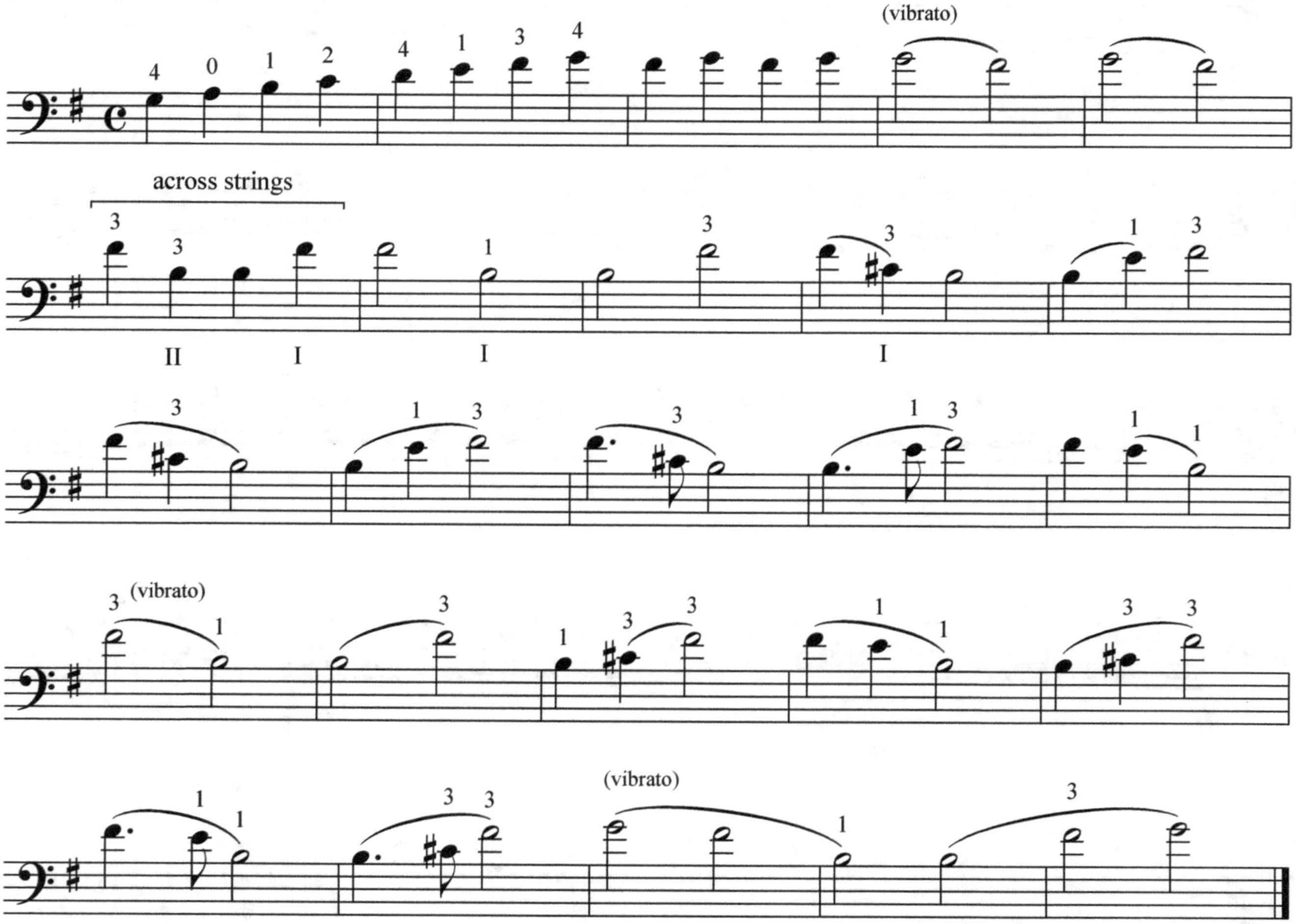

Also available from www.charveypublications.com: CHP349
The Saint-Saens Cello Concerto No. 1 Study Book, Vol. 1

Concerto
Section One: Measures 1-7

Concerto, by Camille Saint-Saëns
Exercises by Cassia Harvey

Learning the Notes and the First Shift
Measures 1, 5

©2019 C. Harvey Publications All Rights Reserved.

www.ingramcontent.com/pod-product-compliance
Lightning Source LLC
Chambersburg PA
CBHW081121080526
44587CB00021B/3698